Caramel

recipes for deliciously gooey desserts

by Peggy Cullen

photographs by Maren Caruso

CHRONICLE BOOKS

SAN FRANCISCO

Library of Congress Cataloging-in-Publication
Data available.

ISBN 0-8118-3647-9

Manufactured in China.

Design by **Jennifer West**
Prop and food styling by **Erin Quon** and **Kim Konecny**
Photo Assistance by **Faiza Ali**

Distributed in Canada by Raincoast Books
9050 Shaughnessy Street
Vancouver, British Columbia V6P 6E5

10 9 8 7 6 5 4 3 2 1

Chronicle Books LLC
85 Second Street
San Francisco, California 94105

www.chroniclebooks.com

for Andy Matlow
Sweeter than honey...
and my parents,
Betsie and Gilbert Cullen

Acknowledgments

Working on these recipes, my thoughts often turned to my teachers at the Culinary Institute of America: Albert Kumin, Walter Schreyer, and Leo Silverman. Twenty-five years later, I still turn to my tattered and butter-stained notes from their classes. The lessons they taught me form the backbone of my baking knowledge.

Shirley Corriher, author of *Cooking Wise,* was always willing to answer my technical questions. She is a wise and generous advisor. Listening to her soft Southern voice on the phone is a bonus.

Mary An Godshall, managing director of the Sugar Processing Research Institute, was instrumental in helping me understand sucrose on a molecular level. After sending me research papers and offering the names of other contacts, she led me to Maurice Jeffrey, consultant to the confectionery industry and chair of the Education and Training Committee of the Pennsylvania Manufacturing Confectioners Association. Mr. Jeffrey patiently enlightened me about, among other things, the Maillard reaction.

Once again, thank you to Bill LeBlond, editorial director, cookbooks, at Chronicle Books, who proposed the idea for this book; his assistant, Amy Treadwell; and my agent, Todd Shuster.

A special thanks to my invaluable tasters, testers, and baking buddies: Patty Burnstein, Peggy Gibbons, Margie Johnson, Marsha Kiesel, Sydell Press, Barbara Price, Laurel Tewes, Diana Ulman, and Sherry Wolff.

The women of the Kitzes family, many gone, are always with me in the kitchen. To them and to my parents, Betsie and Gil Cullen, I owe my baking genes and my love of working with my hands.

I wouldn't have wanted to do this book without the support of my husband, Andy Matlow. Still wearing five chapters from *Got Milk? The Cookie Book* around his middle, he graciously persevered as literary and culinary consultant.

contents

Sweet talk

Making Gold

The word *caramel* describes a color: deep, rich, amber gold. It refers to a flavor: sweet, mellow, and complex. It is also the name of a beloved soft, chewy candy. When we speak of *caramelized sugar*—the golden, flavorful state of almost-burnt sugar—we call that caramel as well.

Caramelized sugar is hot—at least 330°F. Like molten lava, it hardens when cooled. Brittle amber-colored caramel is beautiful. It is as smooth as ice and as transparent as glass. And it is surprisingly versatile. Stir roasted nuts into molten caramel, and you get praline. Add a touch of baking soda, and you have a porous nut brittle. Stir in some heavy cream, butter, or wine, and you get a fluid sauce to pour over ice cream or fruit. Cook it with butter to make a rich toffee candy.

Not all caramel is cooked on the stove top in a skillet or saucepan. The fragile crust that covers crème brûlée is made by melting sugar under a hot broiler or propane torch. Cookies such as palmiers get their golden color and crunchy texture from sugar that caramelizes in the heat of the oven.

From the golden crust of baked bread to the browned skin of roasted chicken, caramelization is responsible for many of the flavors we associate with cooking. All meats and vegetables contain some sugar, in the form of carbohydrates. Roasted in the oven or sautéed in the skillet, the sugar caramelizes, producing the dark color and rich flavor we find so appealing.

The flavor of white granulated sugar—or sucrose—is what scientists refer to as "pure sweet." There are no nuances, no undercurrents of complex flavors, not even an odor. Sugar satisfies our primal craving for sweets, but it is a singular sensation. Caramel, on the other hand, is a complicated collection of tastes and aromas. High heat fragments the sucrose molecule, breaking it down into smaller units that react with each other to form no less than fifty separate flavor components. Caramel is sugar dressed to impress.

Centuries ago, alchemists tried unsuccessfully to make gold. If only they had added sugar to the cauldron, they could have attained their illusive goal—as the pot of clear bubbling syrup morphed into molten golden caramel.

Raising Cane: The Main Ingredient

All green plants produce sugar, or sucrose, when sunlight shines on their leaves. Sugarcane, a giant grass that thrives in the tropics, stores the sugar it produces more readily than any other plant. The sugar beet is the runner-up. Both plants are the source of the white granulated sugar we buy in the supermarket.

When I was a baking major at the Culinary Institute of America twenty-five years ago, I was taught to use cane sugar rather than beet sugar when making caramel. According to my teachers, cane sugar was less likely to crystallize (a generally undesirable reaction wherein the sugar syrup solidifies into a grainy mass).

I've since learned there is little scientific evidence to support this theory, but habit and superstition compel me to use cane sugar exclusively in recipes that contain caramelized sugar. Sugar made from cane is usually labeled as such.

Centuries ago, every sugarcane plantation produced its own sugar. The stone ruins of such plantations are still found throughout the Caribbean. Nowadays, the harvested cane is shipped to mills near the fields, where it is crushed and the juice is extracted. The juice is boiled until a syrupy mass of sugar crystals and molasses develops. They are then separated from each other by centrifugal force. The coarse, brownish sugar that results is called *raw sugar*. Turbinado, Demerara, Muscovado, and other sugars that have a cane or molasses flavor and brownish color are the by-product of these mills and are usually consumed locally.

To remove the impurities and the film of molasses, the raw sugar is shipped to a refinery, often located in another country. (There are eleven sugar refineries in the United States.) What the refiners are after is pure sucrose. To obtain it, the raw sugar undergoes a highly technical process of boiling, filtering, and spinning. Remaining are the fine, granulated, white crystals we know as sugar. It contains no preservatives or additives of any kind.

Light and dark brown sugars are usually refined white sugar that is colored and flavored with molasses syrup. Confectioners' (powdered) sugar is composed of finer particles of refined white sugar combined with a small amount of cornstarch to prevent caking. Sugar in the Raw, the brand name for a coarse, free-flowing light brown sugar found in supermarkets, is turbinado.

Tools and Equipment

General baking equipment is mentioned in the chapter introductions and recipes in which it is used. The following utensils are especially useful for caramelizing sugar.

Heavy saucepan or skillet: To prevent a saucepan or skillet filled with hot caramel from tipping on the stove, it should be heavy. Also, a heavy pan distributes the heat more evenly, preventing hot spots that cause the caramel to burn. Generally, it is not necessary to use a nonstick skillet, unless specified in a recipe. I prefer to caramelize sugar in stainless-steel pans; it's easier to read the color of the caramel as it cooks.

Pastry brush: To prevent the sugar that clings to the side of the pot from crystallizing, it must be washed down using a wet pastry brush. (You can also leave the lid on so that condensation washes the sides of the pot, but I prefer to brush them.) Use a flat brush that doesn't smell of garlic or other ingredients.

Wooden spatula: Used to stir sugar syrup when caramelizing sugar or making candy, wood does not conduct heat to your hand as metal does. A flat-bottomed wooden spatula is preferable to a wooden spoon because it allows you to scrape the corners of the pan, preventing the caramel from burning. Don't use the colorful heat-resistant spatulas sold in cookware stores; they can't always withstand the high temperature required to cook caramel.

Nonbreakable glass: When cooking sugar, always keep a heatproof drinking glass or Pyrex measuring cup filled with water near the stove to hold the pastry brush and wooden spatula. These utensils must be immersed in water each time they are used to wash off any sugar crystals clinging to them. Otherwise, there is the possibility that they could introduce a stray crystal into the pan, seeding a chain reaction that could cause the sugar syrup to crystallize when it cools. Acrylic or Pyrex rather than regular glass is an obvious choice: Accidents happen. Broken glass is no fun to clean up.

Candy thermometer: It's usually not necessary to use a thermometer when caramelizing sugar; simply eyeball the color. When making certain candies, however, a thermometer is essential. If at all possible, use a digital candy/fat thermometer, available through Williams-Sonoma (800-541-2233 or www.williams-sonoma.com). It gives a more accurate reading than a mercury thermometer. (To get a true reading with a mercury thermometer, you must stoop so that your eyes are level with the numbers.) Make sure the bulb or tip of the sensor probe is not touching the bottom of the pot. Most thermometers have a metal casing that extends below the glass tubing for just this purpose. Digital thermometers have a clip that allows the probe to slide up and down. Adjust it accordingly. To test a thermometer, place it in a pot of boiling water; it should read 212°F. To clean off sticky or hardened caramel, place the thermometer in a glass of warm water or run it under hot water. Do not allow the battery case or controls of a digital thermometer to get wet.

Propane torch: The crunchy caramel crust on crème brûlée is achieved by broiling the sugar-topped custard under intense heat. Most home broilers take too long to do the job, heating up the custard in the process. A propane torch, which is sold in hardware stores for about twenty dollars, is a wonderful kitchen tool. It's also terrific for browning meringues. (The smaller, more expensive torches found in cookware stores usually have a flame that is too weak to do a good job.) If you've never used a propane torch, have the hardware store show you how to turn it on, off, and regulate it safely. Be sure there is nothing flammable nearby, such as paper, when you operate it. Keep the flame moving across the surface of the dessert just until it begins to darken.

Baking sheets: Thin metal baking sheets will buckle when hot brittle or buttercrunch is poured onto them. Use baking sheets or sheet pans made with heavy-gauge aluminum or an aluminum-steel combination. Many cookware stores now carry the rimmed sheet pans used by professional bakers. Or order them through the Bakers' catalogue (800-827-6838 or bakerscatalogue.com).

Silicone mats: Usually sold under the name Silpat or Exopat, these reusable, nonstick, silicone-coated baking sheet liners are extremely handy for both caramel and chocolate work. They can withstand high heat and cold temperatures, and nothing sticks to them. You can pour boiling hot brittle, praline, and caramel decorations right onto the mat. Soft caramel-dipped apples or marshmallows can also be placed on a silicone mat, as can candy dipped or coated with tempered chocolate.

Once the caramel or chocolate sets, it peels right off the mat. Wash the mat with soap and water, and hang to dry. Well-stocked cookware stores sell silicone mats. They can also be ordered through the Chef's Catalog (800-338-3232 or chefscatalog.com) or the Bakers' Catalogue (see Baking sheets).

Parchment paper: Professional bakers use sheets of this silicone-coated nonstick paper to line sheet pans. It serves the same purpose as silicone mats but is less expensive. However, it is generally not reusable. Home bakers can purchase rolls of parchment paper at the supermarket. Heavy-grade sheets and rolls can be can also be ordered through Chef's Catalog or the Bakers' Catalogue (see Silicone mats).

Candy-packaging supplies: Soft candies such as turtles and caramel-nut clusters are placed in glassine candy cups to prevent them from sticking to each other. Caramel candies are wrapped in cellophane or waxed paper to help them keep their shape and their stickiness to themselves. These and other supplies, such as wooden sticks for candy apples, gift boxes for candy, and cellophane bags, are available at well-stocked cookware stores or can be ordered through Spectrum Ascona (800-356-1473 or asconapkg.com) or N.Y. Cake & Baking Distributors (800-942-2539).

The basics
and the extras

Turning sugar into caramel is a simple process: Cook it until it turns amber. The chemistry behind this transformation, however, is slightly more complicated.

Like snow, sugar is a crystal. Just as warm weather melts snow into water, heat or moisture dissolves sugar into a liquid called *sugar syrup*. When boiled, the moisture in the sugar begins to evaporate. When enough water evaporates, the sugar starts to turn color. First, it turns a pale honey color, then golden amber, and after that a deep mahogany brown. Left unattended on the stove, sugar smokes and turns black.

Sugar has a strong inclination to return to its original crystalline form. One undissolved sugar crystal can seed a chain reaction that causes the whole batch of sugar syrup to turn grainy. If you've ever ended up with a skillet full of granular, hard white lumps, you know how frustrating this can be.

In some cases, crystallization is desirable. The texture of candies such as fudge and fondant depend on the controlled crystallization of sugar. But generally, it is not a good thing: We want our caramel sauce to be smooth and our peanut brittle to be clear.

Fortunately, there are ingredients that can be added in small quantities to prevent sugar from crystallizing. Sometimes referred to as *doctors* or *interfering agents*, they are acids such as lemon juice, vinegar, and cream of tartar. Liquid sugars such as corn syrup (glucose) and honey, known as *reducing sugars*, help prevent crystallization, as do fatty ingredients such as butter and heavy cream.

Technique also plays a part in preventing crystals from forming. You can wash down the sides of the pot with a wet pastry brush to dissolve any wayward crystals, and refrain from stirring the pot when the sugar syrup is cooking. Follow the instructions on page 16, and you'll never have a problem achieving a clear amber-colored liquid every time you caramelize sugar.

basic recipe for caramelizing sugar

Granulated sugar
Just enough water to moisten the sugar
  (about 1 tablespoon per ¼ cup of sugar)
A few drops of fresh lemon juice or a little
  light corn syrup

1. Set-up: Fill a nonbreakable glass or Pyrex measuring cup with water. Place it next to the stove for storing the pastry brush and wooden spatula when they're not in use. If a recipe calls for plunging the pot of hot caramel into ice water to arrest the cooking, fill a bowl large enough to accommodate the bottom of the pot with ice cubes and water and set aside.

2. Stir: In a clean, heavy skillet or saucepan, gently stir the sugar, water, and lemon juice together.

3. Wash: Using a wet pastry brush, swab down the sides of the pan to wash away any undissolved sugar.

4. Watch: Bring the mixture to a boil and cook, undisturbed, over medium-high heat, until the sugar starts to color around the edges.

5. Swirl: Gently swirl the pan occasionally to even out the color. Continue to cook until it reaches the shade of amber specified in the recipe, 5 to 10 minutes from the time it started boiling—depending on the amount of sugar and the strength of the burner.

6. Remove: Immediately remove the pan from the heat. Plunge the bottom of the pan into a bowl of ice water if the recipe specifies to do so.

Tips and Talk About Caramelizing Sugar

It only takes one undissolved sugar crystal to begin a chain reaction that will turn a batch of caramel into a lumpy mess. Most of the steps taken when caramelizing sugar are meant to prevent crystals from forming:

• Be sure the pan and stirring utensils are clean; sugar crystals form around dirt or foreign particles. Keep the pastry brush and wooden spatula immersed in water when not in use to wash away any undissolved sugar crystals that cling to them.

• A little acid, such as lemon juice, breaks down the sucrose molecules and helps prevent crystals from forming. The exact amount is not crucial: You can simply squeeze a few drops (about ¼ teaspoon) from a wedge of lemon into the pot. Some recipes call for cream of tartar, corn syrup, or honey, which serve the same purpose. It doesn't take much.

• Even gentle stirring to combine the ingredients will splash sugar syrup up on the sides of the pan, where it will cling and possibly form crystals. To dissolve any wayward crystals, wash down the sides of the pan using a wet pastry brush. Alternatively, cover the pan with a lid so that condensation forms as the syrup cooks, which will wash down the insides of the pan. (Be sure to remove the lid when the sugar starts to color so that you can watch it closely.) Feel free to wash down the sides of the pan with a pastry brush at any time during the cooking process. Just be aware that the more water you add to the pot, the longer the sugar will take to caramelize.

• Once the sugar syrup begins to boil, do not stir it. The extra agitation could cause the sugar to crystallize. Also, the thickened sugar syrup will coat the utensil, creating unnecessary mess.

• The sugar will begin to caramelize unevenly because of hot spots on the burner and in the pan. Gently swirl the pan to even out the color and prevent portions of the liquid sugar from burning.

• Sugar continues to darken once it is removed from the burner, due to the residual heat in the pan. Plunging the bottom of the pan into ice water arrests the cooking. Chill the pan for only a few seconds; too long, and the caramel will thicken. Prepare the bowl of ice water ahead so it is ready the moment the caramel is removed from the stove.

• Added liquids such as cream, milk, or liquor will cool the hot caramel and stop the cooking; there is no need then to immerse the pan in ice water. Add liquids gradually, at arm's length, as they often cause the hot caramel to bubble and sputter. If the caramel forms clumps when the liquid is added, place the pan back on the heat for a minute or so—just long enough to dissolve it into a liquid again.

• Sugar is *hygroscopic:* It absorbs water like a sponge. This is why caramel decorations such as spun sugar will not hold up in hot, humid weather. When it comes to cleanup, this factor works in our favor. To dissolve caramel on the sides of a pot or skillet, fill it with water and bring it to a boil. The caramel will melt almost instantly.

❧

note: There are two ways to caramelize sugar in a pot: the *wet method* and the *dry method.* The wet method, described previously, means the sugar is first dissolved in a little water. It takes a few minutes for the water to evaporate before the sugar will start to color, but the pan needs less attention, and the caramel will never be lumpy. To caramelize sugar using the dry method: Rub the sugar with a few drops of lemon juice until it has the consistency of damp sand, and cook until golden, stirring frequently. Be attentive when using this method: The sugar caramelizes quickly.

❧

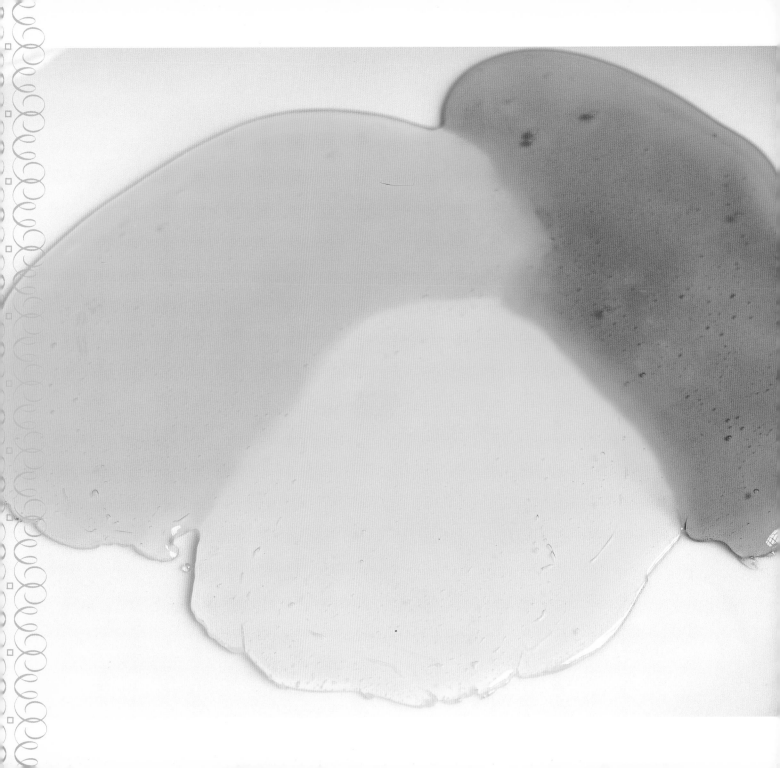

Caramel Color Guide

Cooking sugar is essentially like boiling water: You turn on the heat and wait. The main difference is that when cooking caramel you must be vigilant, or it will burn. The trick is knowing when to stop.

As sugar caramelizes it deepens in color, changing from pale straw to honey gold to an amber brown. It becomes less sweet and more complex in flavor. Depending on how the caramel will be used, the recipe will specify cooking the sugar to a particular hue. There are no official names for these subtle gradations in color. Here, I use the terms *light amber*, *medium amber*, and *dark amber*.

It's rather easy to judge the color of caramel in a stainless-steel pan. If you're not sure, however, examine the caramel against a white background. Drop a little onto a white plate or dip the corner of a sturdy piece of white paper into the hot syrup.

Keep a watchful eye on the color as the caramel cooks. In a matter of seconds, caramel can cross the line from flavorful dark amber to bitter and burned.

When deciding when to remove the pan from the heat, err on the side of too light. Caramel continues to darken once removed from the burner, due to the residual heat in the pan. To halt the cooking process, plunge the bottom of the pan into a bowl of ice water for a few seconds.

If the caramel does get too dark, throw it out and start over. It doesn't take long to cook another batch. Just place the pan of darkened sugar in the sink and run hot water into it. The caramel will dissolve in no time, and you can begin again.

Caution: Hot Caramel

Sugar caramelizes between 320° and 350°F—more than 100° hotter than boiling water. Follow these guidelines to avoid accidents:

· Caramelize sugar in a heavy saucepan or skillet that will not tip on the stove.

· Stir caramel with a wooden utensil; metal conducts heat to your hand.

· Wear a bib apron; it offers extra protection from the occasional splatter.

· Do not taste caramel when it's molten; do not stick your fingers in the pan.

· Use oven mitts or pot holders, especially when handling pans or baking molds into which hot caramel is poured—as when making desserts such as crème caramel (flan).

• Hot caramel steams and sputters when a liquid, such as heavy cream, is added. Add liquids gradually and at arm's length.

• If your skin comes in contact with molten caramel, *immediately rinse the burned area with cold (not iced) water.* If you have the presence of mind, quickly wipe the caramel on your apron or a dish towel before rinsing it to detach it from your skin and prevent it from burning more deeply. Do not apply ice, butter, margarine, or petroleum jelly to burns. Once the pain stops, you can apply a soothing ointment and a dry, sterile dressing.

• When the burn penetrates to deeper layers, characterized by swelling and blistering, it is a *second-degree burn.* Immerse the burned area in cold *(not iced)* water or apply a cool compress until the pain is relieved; do not apply salves or ointments. Consult your doctor or get yourself to a hospital emergency room. With *third-degree burns,* which are rare, the skin appears white or charred; sometimes there is no pain due to nerve damage. Call 911. Try to keep the burned area elevated above the level of the heart.

• Cooking caramel is not an activity for small children; older kids must be closely supervised.

Caramel Cleanup

There is no need to waste time scrubbing caramel that has hardened in a saucepan or skillet or on a utensil. Simply place them in the sink and soak in warm water—the caramel will eventually dissolve. To clean a mercury candy thermometer crusted with caramel, place it in a glass of warm water.

The only exception to this method of cleaning is a digital thermometer or any electric tool; the battery case and controls cannot be immersed in water. To clean a digital thermometer, hold only the probe end under warm running water for a minute or so, until the caramel melts.

To dissolve especially stubborn caramel inside a pan or skillet, fill it with water and boil on the stove for a minute or so. The caramel will melt.

classic caramel dessert sauce

I like to keep a container of this sauce in the fridge at all times to dress up vanilla ice cream, drizzle over fresh fruit, or spoon over warm apple pie or peach cobbler.

Molten caramelized sugar hardens like a lollipop when it cools to room temperature. But if liquid is added to the hot caramel, it remains permanently fluid: It becomes a sauce. Wine, water, butter, liquor, or fruit juice are some of the liquids that can be added to make a flavored caramel sauce. Heavy cream, however, is the classic addition. Creamy caramel sauce goes with just about everything from fruit to nuts and from chocolate cake to cream puffs.

This recipe contains equal parts sugar and cream. It makes an all-purpose sauce that is thin when piping hot, but cools to a thicker fluid at room temperature. For an even thicker, more viscous sauce, good for ice cream sundaes and glazing cakes, double the proportion of sugar to cream (see page 24).

Stir in the heavy cream gradually, at arm's length. Hot caramel bubbles and spits when combined with liquid.

Makes ³/₄ cup

1/2 cup sugar
2 tablespoons water
1 tablespoon light corn syrup
1/2 cup heavy cream
1 tablespoon unsalted butter
1/2 teaspoon pure vanilla extract

To make the caramel: In a small, heavy saucepan, stir the sugar, water, and corn syrup together. Using a wet pastry brush, wash down the sides of the pan. Bring to a boil over medium-high heat and cook undisturbed until the sugar starts to color around the edges. Gently swirl the pan to even out the color and continue to cook until the mixture turns a medium amber. Immediately remove the pan from the heat.

At arm's length, gradually stir in the heavy cream; it will bubble up. Put the pan back on the heat and bring to a boil; remove immediately and stir until the caramel is smooth. Stir in the butter and vanilla extract.

To do ahead: Caramel sauce can be covered and refrigerated for at least 4 days or until the sell-by date stamped on the cream carton. Gently reheat it in the microwave or over low heat on the stove, stirring occasionally. The sauce will be quite stiff when cold and will thin as it warms.

⟳

note: For a larger amount of sauce, double or triple the recipe. Use a medium saucepan to caramelize 1 cup of sugar.

⟳

nut praline

In America—outside of Creole cooking—praline refers to toasted nuts that are coated in golden caramelized sugar. It can be coarsely chopped for a glittering garnish or finely ground and used to flavor desserts. Praline is essentially nut brittle—without the baking soda to lighten the texture.

The term praline *is a bit confusing. In New Orleans, it refers to a patty-shaped candy made with brown sugar and pecans. Throughout Europe, it often refers to any candy with a coating. An English tome,* The New International Confectioner, *describes it as "croquant that has passed through rollers to produce a smooth paste."*

To make praline, whole toasted nuts are stirred into the molten caramel, then poured out to cool, where the mixture hardens into a slab of clear amber candy. As with brittle, you can use any type of nut. For a flavorful praline, be sure to use toasted unsalted nuts. Taste them first; if the nuts aren't flavorful, the praline won't be either.

Generally, the proportion of sugar to nuts is equal: 1 cup of nuts per 1 cup of sugar. But there may be cases where it is desirable to use a little less sugar. The recipe below is standard. Use this technique whenever a recipe calls for praline, but refer to the exact proportions in each recipe.

Makes 1 cup

1/2 cup sugar
2 tablespoons water
1/4 teaspoon fresh lemon juice
1/2 cup hazelnuts, toasted and skinned,
  or almonds, pecans, walnuts, or pine nuts,
  toasted (see facing page)

Lightly butter a baking sheet or line it with parchment paper or a silicone mat.

To caramelize the sugar: In a small, heavy saucepan, stir the sugar, water, and lemon juice together. Using a wet pastry brush, wash down the sides of the pan. Bring to a boil over medium-high heat and cook, undisturbed, until the sugar starts to color around the edges. Gently swirl the pan to even out the color and continue to cook until the mixture turns a medium amber. Immediately remove the pan from the heat.

Stir in the toasted nuts and quickly pour the mixture onto the prepared baking sheet. Use a wooden spatula to press the praline so that it's no more than 1 nut deep. Let cool completely.

Break the praline according to the recipe: Place a piece of waxed paper over a cutting board to catch the pieces. For large shards, break it with your hands. Use a long sharp knife to cut the praline into chunks. If the praline is going to be folded into a dough or batter, place it in a self-sealing plastic bag and gently tap it with the end of a rolling pin. For finer pieces and praline powder, break the slab of candy into pieces and pulse it in a food processor.

To do ahead: If the weather is dry, store the praline for up to 1 week at room temperature on a baking sheet lined with parchment paper or waxed paper. Cover loosely with aluminum foil or parchment paper.

lightning nut praline

This is a quick way to make sweet, crunchy praline with nuts or seeds. You don't need to caramelize the sugar on the stove—it caramelizes in the oven as the nuts toast. Simply moisten the nuts with a minimal amount of egg white, toss them in sugar, and bake in the oven.

Sprinkle these sugar-coated nuts over ice cream sundaes, between layers of cake, or eat them out of hand. If the weather is dry, Lightning Nut Praline will stay crisp for weeks.

Makes about 1¹/3 cups

1 cup untoasted nuts or seeds
1 large egg white
2 tablespoons sugar

Preheat the oven to 350°F. Line a baking sheet with parchment paper or a silicone mat. Place the nuts or seeds in a bowl. In a cup, lightly beat the egg white with a fork until foamy. Stirring with your fingers, add just enough egg white to the nuts to moisten them. If you add too much by mistake, blot the nuts with a paper towel. Toss with the sugar. Spread them out on the prepared baking sheet. Bake for about 6 minutes, then turn the nuts with a metal spatula and bake 2 to 3 minutes more, or until the sugar lying loose on the parchment paper begins to turn golden. Toward the end, check often; don't let the nuts get too dark. Set aside to cool. Separate any clumps sticking together.

toasting nuts

Preheat the oven to 350°F. Spread the nuts in one layer on a rimmed baking sheet. Baking time will vary depending on the type and amount of nuts. Pine nuts toast quickly; hazelnuts, which are dense, take longer. Pecans and walnuts are somewhere in between. It takes about 6 minutes to toast ¹/₂ cup of nuts; 2 cups or more can take 10 to 12 minutes. Shake or stir the nuts once or twice for even toasting. Keep a watchful eye on the color and pay attention to the aroma; you can almost smell when the nuts are ready.

toasting and skinning hazelnuts

Toast in a pre-heated 350°F oven for 10 to 12 minutes until the outer skins blister and split. Place the nuts on a dry towel and rub vigorously to remove the skins. Alternatively, place the warm hazelnuts in a zippered mesh laundry bag and rub them over the kitchen sink. The holes in the bag are big enough to let the skins fall through, but small enough to contain the hazelnuts.

double-dense caramel sauce

The double here refers to the proportion of sugar to heavy cream. There is twice as much as in Classic Caramel Dessert Sauce (page 21), resulting in a thicker liquid. It's especially good over ice cream because it doesn't run down the sides of the scoop so quickly—it drips luxuriously.

Like all caramel, this sauce thickens considerably as it cools. It can be made ahead and refrigerated. For a warm sauce to serve over ice cream, reheat it for a few seconds in the microwave or on the stove over low heat.

Cook the caramel a shade lighter than you ultimately want. Once the cream is stirred in, it will darken in color.

Makes 1 cup

1 cup sugar
1/4 cup water
1/4 teaspoon fresh lemon juice
1/2 cup heavy cream
1/2 teaspoon pure vanilla extract

To make the caramel: In a small, heavy saucepan, stir the sugar, water, and lemon juice together. Using a wet pastry brush, wash down the sides of the pan. Bring to a boil over medium-high heat and cook undisturbed until the sugar starts to color around the edges. Gently swirl the pot to even out the color and continue to cook until the mixture turns a light amber. Immediately remove the pan from the heat.

At arm's length, gradually stir in the heavy cream; it will bubble up. Stir until the caramel is smooth. When the bubbles subside, stir in the vanilla extract.

To do ahead: Caramel sauce can be covered and refrigerated for at least 4 days or until the sell-by date stamped on the cream carton. Gently reheat it in the microwave or over low heat on the stove, stirring occasionally. The sauce will be quite stiff when cold and will thin as it warms.

creamy caramel coating

This soft, chewy, vanilla-flavored caramel is used to coat such gooey delights as caramel apples and turtles. Caramel coating has a wonderful complexity of flavor as well as a malleable, almost plastic, consistency.

The sugar syrup is "enriched" with heavy cream and butter; all the ingredients are cooked together to the *soft-ball stage: 234˚ to 246˚F. As the moisture in the liquids evaporates, the solids become more concentrated. The exact temperature to which the mixture is cooked determines the texture of the caramel. The lower end of the scale yields a caramel that is soft and oozy; the high end results in a caramel that could break your braces.*

Don't be intimidated by a recipe that requires a candy ther-mometer. It's as easy as taking your own temperature. But remember: Each degree counts. If you wear reading glasses, use them here so you can decipher the small lines on the thermometer. Better yet, use a digital candy thermometer (see page 11).

Makes about 2 cups

1 cup sugar
2 tablespoons water
1/2 teaspoon fresh lemon juice
1 cup heavy cream
1/4 teaspoon salt
1 cup light corn syrup
1/4 cup (1/2 stick) unsalted butter,
   cut into pieces
1 teaspoon vanilla extract

Fill a bowl large enough to accommodate the bottom of the pot half full with ice water.

To make the caramel: In a heavy, medium saucepan, gently stir 1/2 cup of the sugar, the water, and lemon juice together. Using a wet pastry brush, wash down the sides of the pan. Bring to a boil over medium-high heat and cook, undisturbed, occasionally washing down the sides of the pan, until the sugar starts to color around the edges. Gently swirl the pot to even out the color and continue to cook until the mixture turns a light amber. Immediately remove the pan from the heat and, at arm's length, gradually stir in the heavy cream; it will bubble up.

Add the remaining 1/2 cup sugar, the salt, corn syrup, and butter to the mixture. Cook over low heat, stirring occasionally, until the caramel dissolves and the butter melts. Wash down the sides of the pan again with a wet pastry brush and increase the heat to medium-high. Insert a thermometer and cook until the temperature reaches anywhere from 234˚ to 246˚ F—according to the recipe in which the coating is used—6 to 8 minutes. Immediately remove the pan from the heat.

Plunge the bottom into the bowl of ice water for a few seconds to stop the cooking. When the bubbles subside, stir in the vanilla. Use immediately or pour into a heatproof container. Let cool, cover, and refrigerate.

To do ahead: Creamy Caramel Coating keeps for up to 2 weeks, covered and refrigerated, due to the fact that the cream is boiled for a few minutes at a high temper-ature. Reheat in a microwave—checking frequently—or over low heat on the stove, stirring occasionally, until fluid, but still thick.

lightly sweetened whipped cream

When making whipped cream, a soft, billowy drift of fluff is what you're after. A dollop should be just firm enough to hold its shape—but not so stiff that it appears grainy. Whether you whisk the heavy cream by hand or beat it with an electric mixer, be sure both the cream and bowl are cold.

The addition of crème fraîche enables the whipped cream to hold its shape over time and helps prevent it from looking grainy. It also adds a subtle sour tang, which can be a welcome foil to a sweet dessert. Add more crème fraîche if you like the flavor. In fact, you can skip the heavy cream altogether and simply sweeten crème fraîche with a little sugar (about 2 tablespoons per cup). Whisk it by hand; it beats up rather quickly and is easy to overwhip when using an electric mixer.

Feel free to adjust the sugar according to your taste. For a flavored topping, add ½ to 1 teaspoon of ground spice, such as cinnamon or ginger, to the liquid cream and sugar.

Makes 2 to 2½ cups

1 cup cold heavy cream
½ cup crème fraîche (optional)
**2 tablespoons granulated sugar
 or 3 tablespoons confectioners' sugar**
1 teaspoon pure vanilla extract

In a deep bowl, combine all the ingredients and beat or whisk until almost—but not quite—stiff.

To do ahead: Whisk or beat the cream until it forms soft peaks. Refrigerate for up to 4 hours. Just before serving, whisk with a few quick strokes to firm it up.

Fruit desserts

caramel-roasted stone fruit

caribbean caramel fruit salad

pears poached in caramel-port syrup

caramel fondue

fresh figs with caramel and crème fraîche

fresh fruit in amber candy coating

Fresh fruit needs sugar when cooked: It loses its natural sweetness in the heat of the oven and fire of the skillet. Caramelized sugar intensifies the flavor, adding not just a simple sweetness, but a complex array of subtle tastes that complement and enhance the innate flavor of the fruit.

The simplest way to combine fresh fruit and caramel is to drizzle a little sauce over ripe, juicy fruit—such as figs or berries—and serve with lightly sweetened crème fraîche. Or, dunk chunks of fruit into a pot of warm caramel sauce or fondue. Boozy caramel syrup makes a lovely marinade for fresh fruit salad. Poached fruit, such as pears simmered in spiced wine, is even tastier when caramelized sugar is used to sweeten the poaching liquid. The juicy fruits of summer, such as peaches, nectarines, plums, apricots, and big fat strawberries, are terrific roasted or sautéed with caramelized sugar. The juice that oozes from the fruit mixes with the amber sugar in the pan, making a lovely dessert sauce that can be extended with heavy cream or butter and poured over the fruit when served. Warm caramel fruit is a splendid sundae topping over a scoop of ice cream.

Other desserts using fruit cooked or baked with caramel are scattered throughout the book:

caramel-roasted stone fruit

In the glory days of summer, there is no lack of luscious, sweet stone fruit such as peaches, plums, nectarines, and apricots. As they are, these fruits are a fine and fitting end to a meal. But it's hard to resist the temptation to tamper. There is nothing like soft, sweet, warm caramel peaches spooned over ice cream or draped over a simple slice of sponge cake.

Roasting these juicy fruits in a bit of caramelized sugar is a quick and easy way to cook them; it softens the flesh and concentrates the natural flavor. A bonus is that once the fruit is cooked, a beautifully flavorful sauce can be made right in the skillet by whisking a little heavy cream into the caramel and exuded fruit juices.

Be sure to cook the caramel on the stove just until it is light amber in color, as it will continue to darken in the oven. When Caramel-Roasted Stone Fruit is served with ice cream or cake, a half piece of fruit is usually enough for 1 person. This dessert is stunning presented in Lacy Caramel Bowls (page 140).

Be sure the fruit you use is sweet and delicious. If the fruit lacks flavor, so will the dessert. For a quick and easy way to sauté sliced summer fruit in caramel, see Caramel-Peach Praline Parfait (page 42).

Makes 8 fruit halves; serves 4 to 8

3/4 cup sugar
3 tablespoons water
1/4 teaspoon fresh lemon juice
4 large ripe but firm peaches or nectarines or plums, or 8 apricots halved and pitted
1/3 cup heavy cream
1/2 teaspoon pure vanilla extract

Lightly Sweetened Whipped cream (page 27), vanilla ice cream, or fruit sorbet for serving

Preheat the oven to 375°F.

To caramelize the sugar: In a heavy 10-inch oven-proof skillet, gently stir the sugar, water, and lemon juice together. Using a wet pastry brush, wash down the sides of the pan. Bring the mixture to a boil over medium-high heat and cook until the sugar starts to color around the edges. Gently swirl the pan to even out the color and continue to cook the mixture until it turns a light amber. Immediately remove the skillet from the heat.

Add the fruit halves, cut-sides down. Put the skillet in the oven and bake for about 5 minutes, or until the caramel darkens and the fruit begins to soften. Using a fork, turn the fruit cut-side up and bake another 3 to 6 minutes, or until it can be pierced easily with a fork. The fruit should be soft, but not falling apart. Note: Apricots cook very quickly; turn them after 3 minutes and watch carefully.

Place an oven mitt over the skillet handle to remind you it's hot. Using a slotted spoon, transfer the fruit to a plate. Whisk the heavy cream into the skillet. Bring it to a boil and immediately remove from the heat. When the bubbles subside, whisk in the vanilla. Let cool for a few minutes to thicken. Meanwhile, use your fingers to slip the skins off the fruit, if you like. Spoon the sauce over the fruit. Serve immediately, with whipped cream or a scoop of ice cream or sorbet.

To do ahead: This dessert is so quick to make you hardly need to prepare it advance. But if you like, roast the fruit and make the sauce in the skillet up to 4 hours ahead. Leave the fruit at room temperature or refrigerate. When ready to serve, heat the sauce over low heat and pour over the fruit and ice cream.

caramel-roasted fruit and summer berries:
Spoon a little sauce into the warm cavities of the fruit and add about 1 cup fresh blueberries, raspberries, and/or blackberries. The heat from the peaches will soften them slightly. Serve with a dollop of whipped cream or ice cream, drizzled with the sauce.

caramel-roasted fruit with fresh herbs:
Perfume the fruit by adding a few sprigs of lavender, rosemary, thyme, lemon verbena, or even basil to the skillet when you make the caramel. Remove before making the sauce. Garnish the roasted fruit with a small sprig of the herb. Serve with whipped cream or ice cream.

caramel-roasted fruit served in an edible bowl:
For a dramatic presentation, fill a Lacy Caramel Bowl (page 140) or Fluted Dessert Bowl (page 105) with the roasted fruit and a scoop of ice cream. Or simply place a few Praline Lace Cigarette Cookies (page 105) on each plate next to the fruit.

caramel-roasted fruit with cake or shortcake:
Top slices of warm Midsummer Cornmeal Cake (page 87), sponge cake, pound cake, or yellow cake with the fruit. Serve with lightly sweetened crème fraîche or ice cream. Or, spoon the fruit over the shortcake, layering the warm fruit with whipped cream.

caramel-roasted fruit sundae:
Top scoops of ice cream with roasted fruit, drizzle with the warm sauce, top with whipped cream, and sprinkle with chopped almond Brittle (page 119).

caramel-roasted fruit with duck or pork:
Serve as a side dish with a savory entrée. Once the fruit is roasted, whisk 1 tablespoon butter into the caramel in place of the heavy cream and vanilla.

caribbean caramel fruit salad

Rum and caramel are an especially good combination, perhaps because they are both by-products of sugarcane. Here, mangoes and papayas—island fruits—are tossed in a simple caramel syrup spiked with rum and flavored with fresh ginger, nutmeg, and lime juice. It's perfect for a Sunday morning breakfast or as a light ending to a heavy meal.

Be judicious with nutmeg—a tiny pinch goes a long way. Use a smooth dark rum such as Gosling's Black Seal or Mount Gay. Cheap rum is rough; no amount of doctoring can make it otherwise.

Serves 6

Caramel-Rum Syrup
1/2 **cup sugar**
2 **tablespoons water**
1/2 **teaspoon fresh lemon juice**
1/3 **cup good-quality dark rum**
1 1/2-**inch piece fresh ginger, peeled and thinly sliced**
1 **cinnamon stick, cracked**
Grating of fresh nutmeg
1 **lime**

3 **ripe mangoes, peeled and cut in** 1/2-**inch cubes**
3 **papayas, peeled, seeded, and sliced in** 1/2-**inch cubes**

To make the syrup: In a small, heavy saucepan, stir the sugar, water, and lemon juice together. Using a wet pastry brush, wash down the sides of the pan. Bring to a boil over medium-high heat and cook, undisturbed, until the mixture starts to color around the edges. Gently swirl the pot to even out the color and continue to cook until the mixture turns a medium amber. Immediately remove the pan from the heat.

At arm's length, gradually stir in the rum; it will bubble up. Stir until the caramel is smooth. Pour into a heatproof container. Add the ginger, cinnamon stick, and nutmeg. Set aside for at least 4 hours or as long as overnight. It will thicken considerably.

Zest the lime using a zester, so that you get thin, curly threads of green zest. In a small saucepan, cover the zest with water, bring it to a boil, and simmer for 5 minutes; drain. Set aside. Squeeze the juice from half of the lime into the caramel syrup and stir to thin the syrup. Place the cut fruit in a bowl and strain the caramel syrup over it, catching the ginger, cinnamon stick, and lime seeds. Add the blanched lime zest to the fruit and gently toss. Refrigerate until ready to serve.

To do ahead: Make the marinade 1 day ahead. Assemble the fruit salad and refrigerate for up to 4 hours.

pears poached in caramel-port syrup

Pears gently simmered in spiced wine make a lean and lovely dessert. This version is a fine example of how caramelized sugar adds nuance and depth to a simple classic. Molten, amber sugar is thinned with ruby port wine to make a poaching liquid for the pears.

Serve the pears in a puddle of caramel-flavored wine syrup with hazelnut or almond Brittle sprinkled in the cavity. To add a rich, sensuous sauce, whip up a fluffy sabayon made with egg yolks, sugar, and wine. Here, the Caramel-Port Syrup is whisked into the yolks for a delicately flavored, billowy sauce.

Make sure to use tasty pears. If they lack flavor, don't even bother poaching them. Bartlett pears, when firm and ripe, are my choice for this dessert, but Bosc or Anjou are also good. An inexpensive ruby port works just fine here. You can also substitute a white Riesling wine.

Serves 6

Caramel-Port Syrup
2 cups sugar
1/2 cup water
1 teaspoon fresh lemon juice
3 cups ruby port wine
1 vanilla bean, split lengthwise
2-inch piece fresh ginger, peeled and thinly sliced
3 star anise pods or 1/2 teaspoon aniseed, crushed
2 bay leaves
1 cinnamon stick, broken

3 firm, ripe pears, about 1 1/2 pounds, peeled, cored, and halved

Caramel-Port Sabayon
3 large egg yolks
2/3 cup warm Caramel Port Syrup (above)
1/2 cup heavy cream

1/2 recipe hazelnut Brittle or almond Brittle (page 119), optional

To make the syrup: In a heavy saucepan wide enough to accommodate 6 pear halves (about 8 inches in diameter), stir the sugar, water, and lemon juice together. Using a wet pastry brush, wash down the sides of the pan. Bring to a boil over medium-high heat and cook, undisturbed, until the sugar starts to color around the edges. Gently swirl the pot to even out the color and continue to cook until the mixture turns a light amber. Immediately remove the pan from the heat.

(continued)

At arm's length, add the wine—it will boil and sputter. Using a small knife, scrape the seeds from the vanilla pod into the liquid; add the pod as well. Stir in the ginger, star anise, bay leaves, and cinnamon stick.

Bring the syrup to a boil, reduce heat to a simmer, and add the pear halves. Cook, uncovered, turning the pears occasionally, for 10 to 20 minutes, or until a knife inserted into the fruit offers no resistance. Using a slotted spoon, transfer the pears to a bowl. Return the syrup to medium-low heat and simmer, uncovered, for about 15 minutes or until reduced to about 2 cups.

To make the sabayon: In a medium stainless-steel bowl, beat the egg yolks with a whisk or handheld electric mixer while gradually adding ²⁄₃ cup of the warm syrup. Set the bowl over a saucepan filled with 1 inch of barely simmering water. (The bottom of the bowl should not touch the water.) Beat or whisk constantly for 6 to 10 minutes, or until the mixture is thick and fluffy and mounds softly when dropped from the beater. Remove from the heat and whisk until completely cool, 3 to 5 minutes. Whip the cream until it forms soft peaks. Using a rubber spatula, fold it into the sabayon.

Serve the pears warm or at room temperature. Pour a few tablespoons of the caramel-wine syrup into each of 6 shallow bowls. Spoon a few large dollops of sabayon over the syrup and top with a pear half, cut-side up. Drizzle more syrup over the pear. If you like, sprinkle the cavity with some brittle. Place the remaining syrup in a small pitcher to pass at the table.

To do ahead: Poach the pears 1 day ahead. Store, refrigerated, in some of the syrup. (Juices from the pears will dilute the thick syrup, so reserve most of the syrup separately.) The sabayon with the whipped cream folded in can be covered and refrigerated for up to 1 day.

caramel fondue

Fondue is communal food—a shared pot of warm sauce for dipping and coating all sorts of delicacies. Here, the pot is filled with a thick, golden caramel sauce; the "dip-ins" are sliced apples, bananas, peaches, pears, or pineapple. Go a bit over the top—so to speak—by coating the sticky caramel-draped morsels in a choice of chopped nuts, grated chocolate, or toasted coconut.

When you're hosting a crowd, this is a quick and easy dessert to prepare. The caramel takes only minutes on the stove; it can be made ahead and reheated in the microwave for a few seconds or on the stove over low heat.

Present this fondue as the centerpiece (and conversation piece) of your after-dinner coffee and chitchat. Or serve it buffet-style, like a dessert version of crudités and dip.

Makes 2½ cups

Dipping Caramel
1½ cups sugar
½ cup water
¼ cup light corn syrup
¾ cup heavy cream
1½ teaspoons pure vanilla extract

Fresh lemon juice for drizzling
Chunks, slices, or thick wedges of bananas, pineapple, peaches, pears, apricots, and/or apples
½ cup *each* finely chopped nuts, grated chocolate, and/or toasted coconut for toppings (optional)

To make the caramel: In a heavy 2- or 3-quart saucepan, stir the sugar, water, and corn syrup together. Using a wet pastry brush, wash down the sides of the pan. Bring to a boil over medium-high heat and cook, undisturbed, until the sugar starts to color around the edges. Gently swirl the pan to even out the color and continue to cook the mixture until it turns a light amber. Immediately remove the pan from the heat.

At arm's length, gradually stir in the heavy cream; it will bubble up. Stir until the caramel is smooth. When the bubbles subside, stir in the vanilla. Set aside to cool and thicken for at least 30 minutes, whisking occasionally.

Meanwhile, drizzle a little lemon juice over the fruit to prevent it from browning. Set a bowl on a platter and arrange the fruit around it. If including the toppings, place them in small bowls to the side. Whisk the caramel with a few quick strokes and pour it into the bowl. Use bamboo skewers or fondue forks to dip the fruit.

To do ahead: Make the caramel up to 2 days ahead, cover, and refrigerate. Reheat just before serving. Slice the fruit up to 3 hours before serving, drizzle with fresh lemon juice, cover loosely with plastic wrap, and refrigerate. Leftover caramel can be reheated and used as a warm dessert sauce for ice cream or cake.

fresh figs with caramel and crème fraîche

My first job in New York City, in 1980, was working for the caterer Glorious Foods. It was June: fig season. One of the insanely simple desserts the chef frequently served his society clientele was a plate of fresh black figs, cut open like flowers to reveal their sensuous pink centers, with raspberries and crème fraîche on the side.

This is still one of my favorite flavor combinations. Drizzled with caramel, a glorious dessert is even more so. It's a quick, light summer dessert. Substitute thick slices of fresh juicy peaches or apricots for the figs, if you like. For a striking presentation, serve this dessert in Lacy Caramel Bowls (page 140).

Serves 6

Classic Caramel Dessert Sauce (page 21)
Lacy Caramel Bowls (page 140), optional
1½ cups crème fraîche
2 tablespoons sugar
**1 vanilla bean, split lengthwise, or 1 teaspoon
   pure vanilla extract**
18 large ripe figs, stemmed
1 cup fresh raspberries

Make the caramel sauce and set aside to cool. Make the caramel bowls, if you're using them.

In a medium bowl, beat together the crème fraîche, sugar, and the seeds from the vanilla bean or vanilla extract until the mixture forms soft peaks. Be careful not to overbeat. Set aside.

Halve and then quarter each fig lengthwise without slicing through the base of the fruit, leaving the 4 sections attached. Spread the sections open like the petals of a flower.

Puddle a little caramel sauce on each of 6 dessert plates. Place 3 large figs on each and scatter raspberries in and around the figs. Place a large dollop of sweetened crème fraîche next to the figs and drizzle with more caramel. Alternatively, arrange the ingredients in 6 caramel bowls. Serve immediately.

To do ahead: Make the caramel dessert sauce up to 3 days ahead and refrigerate. Reheat and cool slightly before serving. The caramel bowls can also be made 1 day ahead, if the weather is dry.

note: Crème fraîche is available in fine food stores and supermarkets, in the cheese or dairy department.

fresh fruit in amber candy coating

Beautiful to behold, these glittering, golden candy-coated fruits taste as good as they look. Bite down on the delicate, brittle shell to revel the soft, juicy fruit inside. Serve these fruits as a simple sweet centerpiece or as a garnish for another dessert.

Whole strawberries, figs, tangerine slices, and even large grapes may be dipped into molten caramel. Hung off skewers to set, the caramel drips off the tip of the fruit in long, whimsical threads. Whole nuts may be coated in the same fashion.

Moisture dissolves caramel, so be sure that both the work area and the fruit are completely dry. Dip the fruit in the caramel as close to serving as possible. Use only whole soft fruits or whole segments (as with tangerines), not slices.

Makes 15 to 18 pieces

15 to 18 fresh figs or large strawberries, green stem ends left on, or other fruit (see headnote)
1 cup sugar
1/4 cup water
1/2 teaspoon fresh lemon juice

Completely dry the bottom of the kitchen sink. Using bamboo skewers, pierce each fruit or berry crosswise near the widest end, so that the fruit hangs at a right angle off the skewer. Fill a bowl large enough to accommodate the bottom of a small saucepan half full with ice water.

To make the caramel: In a small saucepan, gently stir the sugar, water, and lemon juice together. Using a wet pastry brush, wash down the sides of the pan. Bring the mixture to a boil over medium-high heat until the sugar starts to color around the edges. Gently swirl the pan to even out the color and continue to cook the mixture until it turns a light amber. Immediately remove the pot from the heat.

Plunge the bottom into the bowl of ice water for about 8 seconds to stop the cooking. Remove the pot from the water and wipe the bottom of the pot dry. The caramel is cool enough to dip when it drips off a fork in a steady thread. Holding the fruit by the end of the bamboo skewer, tilt the pot and dip the fruit in the warm caramel, covering it at least halfway.

Secure the end of the bamboo skewer to the counter with a piece of tape so that the fruit is extended out over the sink. Allow the caramel to drip in a long string off the bottom tip of the fruit. Meanwhile, dip the next piece.

Reheat the caramel over low heat when it becomes too cool and thick to work with. When the caramel on the fruit is set, remove the skewers and place the fruit—wide, undipped-ends down—on a plate.

To do ahead: Caramelize the sugar and pour it in a puddle onto a piece of parchment paper or silicone mat. Let it cool and harden. If the weather is dry, the caramel will keep indefinitely. Store at room temperature on a baking sheet lined with parchment paper or aluminum foil. Melt the caramel in a pot over low heat when you are ready to dip the fruit.

Ice cream desserts

With so many wild and crazy concoctions in the supermarket freezer case, there's not much need to make caramel ice cream from scratch. But you can use caramel—in all its forms—to transform scoops of store-bought into lavish sundaes and parfaits.

Sauté sliced fruit with caramelized sugar; it makes its own caramel-fruit sauce right in the skillet. Spoon warm, syrupy caramel peaches or bananas over ice cream. Stir nuts into caramelized sugar to make crunchy brittle to scatter over an ice cream parfait. The contrast in textures between smooth, soft ice cream and porous nut brittle is especially pleasing. And of course, there's warm caramel sauce. Poured over ice cream and topped with whipped cream, plain vanilla ice cream becomes a sublime sundae.

To save time when serving to company, scoop the ice cream up to 1 day ahead. Place the scoops on a plate or small baking sheet lined with waxed paper and store in the freezer until completely hardened, about 20 minutes. Cover with plastic wrap to prevent ice crystals from forming. This speeds serving when you're ready to assemble the sundaes.

caramel-peach praline parfait

This is the perfect dessert for a hot summer night when you can't bear to turn on the oven. Caramelize sugar in the skillet, add sliced peaches, and sauté until tender. The juices of the fruit mingle with the caramel to make a silky, fruit-flavored caramel sauce. With no added butter or heavy cream, this is a lovely, light fruit topping. Sliced nectarines or plums can be substituted for the peaches.

If you're in the mood to do something special, present this parfait in a Lacy Caramel Bowl (page 140) or a Fluted Dessert Bowl (page 105). Caramel-Sautéed Peaches are also wonderful spooned over Midsummer Cornmeal Cake (page 87).

For a light crunchy topping, Lightning Nut Praline (page 23) is a quick and easy way to toast and sweeten pecans. It requires less than a minute of preparation plus a few minutes of baking.

Serves 4

Caramel-Sautéed Fruit
1/2 cup sugar
2 tablespoons water
1/2 teaspoon fresh lemon juice
3 large, ripe but firm peaches, nectarines, or plums, or 4 apricots, pitted and cut into 1/2-inch slices (see headnote)

1 pint vanilla, caramel swirl, or butter pecan ice cream
Lightly Sweetened Whipped Cream (page 27)
1/2 recipe Lightning Nut Praline, made with pecans, coursely chopped (optional)

To make the Caramel-Sautéed Fruit: In a heavy, medium skillet, gently stir the sugar, water, and lemon juice together. Using a wet pastry brush, wash down the sides of the pan. Bring to a boil over medium-high heat and cook, undisturbed, until the sugar starts to color around the edges. Gently swirl the pan to even out the color and cook until the mixture turns a medium amber.

Add the sliced peaches. Cook for about 2 minutes on one side, then turn and continue to cook for another 1 to 4 minutes or until tender but not mushy. Remove from the heat. Transfer the peaches and sauce to a bowl so that they don't continue to cook.

Scoop the ice cream into 4 parfait glasses or shallow dishes. Spoon the warm peaches and caramel sauce over the ice cream. Garnish with a dollop of whipped cream and sprinkle with the praline, if you like.

To do ahead: If the weather is dry, the praline can be made up to 3 days ahead and stored at room temperature, lightly covered with aluminum foil or parchment paper.

Peeling Peaches: If you prefer peeled peaches, blanch and skin the fruit before slicing. Immerse a few peaches at a time in a large saucepan of boiling water for about 30 seconds. Remove with a slotted spoon and run under cold water. The skins will slip right off.

caramel hot fudge sauce

Hot caramel and cream stirred into bittersweet chocolate make a thick and gooey ice cream sauce. Keep it on hand, refrigerated. When the craving for a hot fudge sundae strikes, reheat it carefully for a few seconds in the microwave or over low heat, stirring. To make a large amount, simply double the recipe.

Makes 1 cup, enough for about 6 sundaes

1/2 cup sugar
2 tablespoons water
1 tablespoon light corn syrup
1/2 cup heavy cream
5 ounces high-quality bittersweet chocolate, finely chopped
1/2 teaspoon pure vanilla extract

To caramelize the sugar: In a small, heavy saucepan, stir the sugar, water, and corn syrup together. Using a wet pastry brush, wash down the sides of the pan. Bring to a boil over medium-high heat and cook, undisturbed, until the sugar starts to color around the edges. Gently swirl the pot to even out the color and continue to cook until the mixture turns a medium amber. Immediately remove the pan from the heat.

At arm's length, gradually stir in the heavy cream. Add the finely chopped chocolate. Let sit for 1 minute to melt the chocolate, then gently stir to combine. Stir in the vanilla. Transfer to a heatproof container. Let sauce cool until it thickens but is still slightly warm.

To do ahead: Make up to 4 days ahead and refrigerate. Reheat for a few seconds in the microwave or on the stove over low heat, stirring. Using a small whisk or fork, beat with several quick strokes.

caramelized banana split-second sundae

Like Caramel-Peach Praline Parfait (page 42), this sundae offers instant gratification without fussing in the kitchen. Bananas and caramel are a classic combination—they create their own harmony. Here, they're served warm over ice cream with a creamy banana-flavored caramel sauce that's made right in the skillet from the fruit drippings.

If you serve this for company, prepare it right before serving. It cooks so quickly, you'll miss only a minute or so of after-dinner table talk.

Be sure to use firm bananas. Soft fruit will disintegrate before it's cooked.

Serves 6

3 large, ripe but firm bananas
2 tablespoons (¼ stick) unsalted butter
1 tablespoon light corn syrup
½ cup sugar
⅓ cup heavy cream
1 to 2 pints premium vanilla ice cream
Lightly Sweetened Whipped Cream (page 27), optional
Freshly grated nutmeg

Cut the bananas in half crosswise, then cut each piece in half lengthwise. Set aside. In a heavy, medium skillet, melt the butter over low heat. Stir in the corn syrup and the sugar. Increase the heat to medium-high and cook, stirring occasionally and washing down the sides of the pan with a wet pastry brush, until the mixture turns golden, about 2 minutes. Don't let it darken. It's okay if the butter separates. Immediately remove the skillet from the heat and arrange the bananas in the pan, cut-sides up.

Return the skillet to medium-high heat and cook until the undersides of the bananas begin to brown, 1 to 3 minutes. Check them by lifting with a fork. They won't all begin to color at the same time, so keep an eye out for hot spots in the skillet. Once a slice begins to brown, use the fork to flip it. Cook on the second side for a few seconds. To prevent them from turning mushy, it's better to slightly undercook the bananas. Use a fork to transfer 2 banana slices, rounded-sides up, to each of 6 dessert plates or shallow bowls.

When the last slice is done, stir the heavy cream into the skillet. Let it boil, stirring with the fork or a whisk to scrape up all the pan drippings, until the cream is golden, about 1 minute. Immediately strain the caramel into a small bowl.

Scoop the ice cream between the warm bananas and drizzle the caramel sauce over the ice cream (about 1 generous tablespoon per serving). Add a dollop of whipped cream, if you like, and a very light grating of fresh nutmeg. Serve immediately.

caramel brittle sundae

Thick caramel sauce, sugared nuts, warm chocolate sauce, and whipped cream: These are the makings of a classic ice cream sundae. Below are just two variations; pick and choose any of the following components to create your favorite. To have your bowl and eat it, too, serve the ice cream in Fluted Dessert Bowls (page 105) or Lacy Caramel Bowls (page 140). Or ornament your sundae with a glittering, glitzy garnish such as Corkscrews (page 134) or Drips and Drizzles (page 139).

The small amount of baking soda in brittle gives it a porous, slightly softer texture that is much more pleasing with ice cream than the hard crunch of nut praline. Don't be afraid to make brittle; it takes only minutes and is as easy as cooking pasta. Use any nut you please. When cool, cut the brittle into nut-sized pieces, leaving some larger shards with which to garnish the sundae.

Serves 4

1 1/2 pints ice cream of your choice, from simple vanilla to complicated combinations of chocolate, caramel, and/or nut
Caramel Hot Fudge Sauce (page 43)
1/2 recipe Any Nut Brittle (page 119)
Double-Dense Caramel Sauce (page24)
Lightly Sweetened Whipped Cream (page 27)

nutty buddy sundae: When I was growing up, the Good Humor man was our neighborhood Pied Piper. Kids came running from all directions when they heard him ringing his bells. For one whole summer, my favorite was a vanilla cone topped with chocolate and crushed peanuts. Here is a homemade sundae version of that commercial treat: Scoop vanilla ice cream into 4 bowls, top with 1 cup warmed Caramel Hot Fudge Sauce, and sprinkle with chopped Any Nut Brittle made with peanuts. Garnish each with a shard of brittle and top with a dollop of whipped cream.

caramel coffee bar parfait: As evident in coffee bars across the country, we have developed a national passion for the combination of hazelnut and coffee. Caramel enhances both of those flavors. Here, ice cream is topped with warm caramel sauce and crunchy chopped hazelnut brittle. Scoop coffee or vanilla ice cream into 4 parfait glasses. Layer the ice cream with 1 cup barely warmed Double-Dense Caramel Sauce and Any Nut Brittle made with toasted hazelnuts, chopped into pieces about the size of a whole nut. Top with a dollop of whipped cream. For a variation, add or substitute hot fudge sauce for the caramel sauce and substitute pine nuts for the hazelnuts.

baked alaska brittle pie

This is an easy-to-assemble pie version of the fabulous retro dessert baked Alaska. The "crust" is a melt-in-your-mouth flourless chocolate soufflé that puffs up proudly in the oven, then sinks as it cools, creating the perfect cavity in which to mound the ice cream. The chocolate soufflé has the added advantage of remaining light and chewy, even when frozen.

Coarsely chopped pecan brittle is sandwiched between the crust and the ice cream, and the whole thing is slathered with a billowy drift of meringue. Torched, or baked in a very hot oven for just a few minutes, the tips and peaks of the meringue are lightly browned.

Use the elements in this recipe to create your own ice cream–pie extravaganza. Any of the outrageous caramel-flavored ice cream concoctions by Ben & Jerry's or Häagen-Dazs can be layered with almond, hazelnut, or pecan brittle. Mango, passion fruit, or coconut sorbet layered with macadamia or almond brittle is also a heavenly combination.

Makes one 9-inch pie

Chocolate Soufflé Pie
4 ounces high-quality semisweet or bittersweet chocolate, chopped
4 large eggs
1/2 cup sugar
1/8 teaspoon cream of tartar

Any Nut Brittle (page 119), made with pecans or nuts of your choice, coarsely chopped
2 pints caramel-swirl ice cream or sorbet, slightly softened

Meringue Topping
4 large egg whites at room temperature
Pinch of cream of tartar
1 cup sugar
1 teaspoon pure vanilla extract

Classic Caramel Dessert Sauce (page 21)

To make the pie crust: Preheat the oven to 325°F. Melt the chocolate in a double boiler over barely simmering water or in a microwave for about 1 1/2 minutes; set aside. Separate the eggs, putting the whites and yolks in separate mixing bowls. (For beaten egg whites to attain full volume, the bowl must be grease-free. Wipe the inside of the bowl with a paper towel moistened with vinegar to remove any residual fat.)

Using an electric mixer, beat the egg yolks and $\frac{1}{4}$ cup of the sugar until fluffy and pale in color, about 3 minutes. Using a rubber spatula, stir in the melted chocolate. Wash the beaters with soap and warm water; dry thoroughly. Beat the egg whites on medium-high speed until frothy. Add the cream of tartar and continue beating until the whites just begin to form soft peaks. Gradually beat in the remaining $\frac{1}{4}$ cup sugar, a few teaspoons at a time, until stiff, glossy peaks form. Using the rubber spatula, stir one-fourth of the meringue into the chocolate to lighten it. Carefully fold the remaining meringue into the chocolate mixture. Pour the batter into an ungreased 9-inch glass pie plate and shake gently to even. Bake for 30 minutes or until a skewer inserted in the center comes out clean. Transfer to a wire rack to cool completely. The pie will sink as it cools.

Sprinkle the brittle in a thick layer on the bottom of the cooled chocolate pie crust. (There will be some left over.)

Place the ice cream in the bowl of an electric mixer (using the paddle attachment if you have a choice) and mix on low speed for a few seconds until spreadable. Mound the ice cream in the pie shell, press to compress, and freeze for at least 3 hours or as long as overnight. Cover with plastic wrap when completely hard.

Preheat the oven to 500°F if using the oven rather than a propane torch to brown the meringue.

To make the Meringue Topping: Beat the egg whites on medium speed. When frothy, add the cream of tartar and continue beating until the whites just begin to form soft peaks. Beat in the sugar a few tablespoons at a time, gradually increasing the speed to high, until all the sugar is added and stiff, glossy peaks form. Beat in the vanilla.

Using an icing or palette knife, spread a very thin layer of the meringue over the pie to completely cover the ice cream. Using a pastry bag fitted with a number 5 or 6 star tip, pipe the meringue over the pie in a decorative fashion. Alternatively, spread the meringue over the pie and use the back of a spoon to create decorative peaks.

Place the pie on a heavy baking sheet and bake for 2 to 3 minutes, or until the tips of the meringue are browned. Or use a propane torch (see page 12). Freeze for at least 1 hour or overnight. Serve with caramel sauce on the side.

To do ahead: The pie can be assembled and frozen 1 day ahead. Classic Caramel Dessert Sauce can be made up to 3 days ahead.

Tarts, pastries, *and pies*

There are some time-honored traditions for incorporating caramel into pastry desserts. Tarte Tatin, a classic French pastry, is made by cooking apples in a golden mixture of butter and sugar until the fruit renders its juices, absorbing the caramel into its flesh. Flaky pastry turnovers and tartlets filled with apples cooked in this fashion are sublime.

Borrowing from the method used to broil the burnt sugar crust on top of crème brûlée, tarts filled with creamy, soft fillings, such as lemon curd, can also be "brûléed." In fact, crème brûlée tarts, filled with the traditional vanilla-flavored custard, have recently been making their appearance on restaurant menus.

Replace the granulated sugar in old-fashioned favorites like coconut cream pie and strawberry short-cake with caramelized sugar. The familiar and comforting flavors are essentially unchanged, but the sweetness itself is more complex and alluring.

Almost any warm tart or fresh fruit pie is enhanced with a scoop of ice cream or a dollop of whipped cream. Drizzle these creams with Classic Caramel Dessert Sauce (page 21). "On the side" is one of the best ways to enjoy caramel with pastry desserts.

tarte tatin

No matter how many times I make this Tarte Tatin (pro-nounced tart ta-TAN), there is always a feeling of excited awe when the skillet is flipped and removed, revealing concentric circles of glistening caramel-glazed apples. This upside-down apple tart, French in origin, is a classic caramel dessert. Like the two caramelized apple desserts that follow, it is best baked in autumn, when apples are firm and fresh.

Quartered apples are cooked over high heat in a skillet with butter and sugar. As the moisture in the fruit evaporates, the flesh becomes infused with the hot caramel. Once the apples are caramelized to a golden hue, the pan is covered with a round of flaky pastry dough, and the whole thing is baked in the oven until the crust is golden brown. Inverted onto a serving dish, the crunchy crust ends up on the bottom of the tart.

Flaky pastry dough, or pâte brisée, which is quick and easy to make in a food processor, is the best dough for Tarte Tatin. I don't recommend using store-bought puff pastry as a shortcut here—it comes out soggy. Once the dough is positioned over the apples, moisten it lightly and sprinkle heavily with sugar. The sugar will partially caramelize, adding extra crunch to the finished crust.

Makes one 10-inch tart

Flaky Pastry Dough
1 1/4 cups all-purpose flour
1/2 teaspoon salt
1 tablespoon sugar
1/2 cup (1 stick) cold unsalted butter, cut into 1/2-inch dice
3 to 4 tablespoons ice water

8 large baking apples (3 1/2 to 4 pounds total), such as Northern Spy, Ida Red, Jonagold, or Golden Delicious
Juice of 1/2 lemon
4 tablespoons (1/2 stick) unsalted butter
3/4 cup plus 1 tablespoon sugar
Vanilla ice cream or Lightly Sweetened Whipped Cream (page 27) for serving

To make the dough: Combine the flour, salt, and sugar in a food processor. Pulse to mix. Add the butter and pulse until the butter pieces are the size of peas. Remove the lid of the machine and pour 3 tablespoons of the water evenly over the mixture. Pulse a few times to evenly moisten the dough. Squeeze some of the mixture with your hand. If it comes together as a dough, it is done. If it crumbles, add another tablespoon of water and pulse again to mix.

Turn the dough out onto a work surface, it will appear crumbly. Using the heel of your hand, gently mash the dough with a few quick strokes to bring it together. Form it into a disk, cover with plastic wrap, and refrigerate for at least 30 minutes or up to 2 days.

On a lightly floured work surface, roll the dough out into an 11-inch round (1 inch larger than the skillet), lifting it frequently and adding more flour as necessary. If the dough sticks to the work surface, slide a long metal palette knife underneath to release it. Transfer the pastry to a baking sheet lined with waxed or parchment paper. (For easy transfer, fold the round in half, move it to the baking sheet, and then open it.) Cover with plastic wrap and refrigerate until ready to use.

To caramelize the apples: Preheat the oven to 425°F. Peel, core, and quarter the apples, squeezing the lemon juice over them to prevent browning. (To core apples quickly, peel and halve them, then scoop out the centers using a melon baller.) In a heavy 10-inch ovenproof skillet, preferably nonstick, melt the butter over low heat. Add the ³/₄ cup sugar and cook over medium-high heat, stirring occasionally, until the mixture turns a pale golden brown color, 2 to 3 minutes. Don't let it darken. It's okay if the butter separates. Immediately remove the skillet from the heat. Arrange the apples, standing on end, in concentric circles. It helps to use a wooden spoon to support the first apple in the line until you get them all in. It will seem crowded, but just slip the last slices straight down between the apples in the center. They will shrink as they cook.

Place the apples over high heat and cook, undisturbed, for 10 to 12 minutes, or until the undersides are golden and soft but not so soft that they disintegrate. The mixture will boil and bubble. Remove from the heat.

Using a fork, spoon, or the tip of a paring knife, flip each apple slice so that the caramelized end is pointing up. (The easiest way to maneuver the apples is to simply flip each slice so that it's facing the opposite direction.) Cook the apples for another 5 minutes over medium-high heat. Immediately remove the skillet from the heat.

Remove the rolled dough from the refrigerator. Peel away the plastic wrap and center the dough over the skillet. Working quickly, use scissors to trim the edges so that there is an even ¹/₂-inch border of dough extending beyond the edge of the skillet. Being careful not to burn your fingers, tuck the extra dough down between the apples and the skillet; don't be too fussy with this step. Using a wet pastry brush, lightly moisten the surface of the dough. Sprinkle it heavily with the 1 tablespoon sugar. Immediately place in the oven.

Bake for 15 to 20 minutes, or until the crust is golden brown, then lower the temperature to 375°F and bake for another 15 minutes. Remove from the oven and let cool on a wire rack for exactly 5 minutes. Place a large serving dish over the top of the skillet. Using oven mitts, quickly flip the skillet and dish together to invert the tart onto the plate. Slowly remove the skillet. Scrape any apples clinging to the skillet onto the tart. Serve warm, with ice cream or whipped cream.

To do ahead: The dough can be made and frozen for up to 2 weeks. The rolled dough round can be refrigerated on the lined baking sheet, covered with plastic wrap, for up to 1 day.

rustic puff apple tartlets

Caramel and apples are a love match. Cooked together, the caramel is absorbed into the flesh of the fruit, melding the flavors from the inside out. This is because the apple's firm texture enables it to withstand a longer cooking time than softer fruits and berries. As the flesh gives off its juices, it absorbs the caramel in which it stews.

With the technique for caramelizing apples used in the recipe for Tarte Tatin (page 52), you can make an alluring assortment of desserts. The most difficult thing about this recipe is peeling the apples. Use a melon baller to neatly core the apple halves.

These rustic tartlets are a good do-ahead dessert when company is coming. Assemble them early in the day and keep them in the refrigerator, covered. Pop them in the oven when you sit down to dinner. Serve with ice cream or whipped cream on the side and drizzle with Classic Caramel Dessert Sauce.

Makes 8 tartlets

One 17-ounce package frozen puff pastry, thawed
8 large baking apples (3 1/2 to 4 pounds total), such as Northern Spy, Ida Red, Jonagold, or Golden Delicious
Juice of 1/2 lemon
4 tablespoons (1/2 stick) unsalted butter
3/4 cup plus 2 tablespoons sugar
1 large egg beaten with 1 teaspoon water
Vanilla ice cream or Lightly Sweetened Whipped Cream (page 27)
Classic Caramel Dessert Sauce (page 21), warmed (optional)

On a lightly floured surface, gently roll a sheet of puff pastry out into a 12-inch square. Using a sharp knife or a pizza wheel, cut the dough into four 6-inch squares. Cut off the corners of each square so that they are rounded. Repeat with the second sheet of dough. Cover the rounds with plastic wrap and stack them in the refrigerator.

Peel, core, and quarter the apples, squeezing the lemon juice over them to prevent browning. In a heavy 10-inch ovenproof skillet, preferably nonstick, melt the butter over low heat. Add the 3/4 cup sugar and cook over medium-high heat, stirring occasionally, until the mixture turns a pale golden brown, 2 to 3 minutes. Don't let it darken. It's okay if the butter separates. Immediately remove the skillet from the heat. Arrange the apples, standing on end, in concentric circles. It helps to use a wooden spoon to support the first apple in the line until you get them all in. It will seem crowded, but just slip the last slices straight down between the apples in the center. They will shrink as they cook.

Place the apples over high heat for 10 to 12 minutes and cook, undisturbed, until the undersides are golden and soft but not so soft that they disintegrate. The mixture will boil and bubble. Remove from the heat. Using a fork, spoon, or the tip of a paring knife, flip each apple slice so that the caramelized end is pointing up. (The easiest way to maneuver the apples is to simply flip each slice so that it's facing the opposite direction.) Cook for another 5 minutes over medium-high heat. Immediately remove the skillet from the heat. Line a baking sheet with waxed or parchment paper and turn the apples out onto the sheet. Gently separate them and let cool completely.

(continued)

Preheat the oven to 375°F. Cluster 4 apple quarters in the center of each round of dough. Fold the borders of the dough over the apples, pinching and pleating it, leaving an opening in the center. Place the tarts on an ungreased heavy baking sheet.

Using a pastry brush, lightly brush the dough with the egg mixture and sprinkle the tarts with the 2 tablespoons sugar. Bake for 30 minutes, or until golden brown. Place the baking sheet on a wire rack to cool slightly. Serve warm with ice cream or whipped cream. Drizzle with classic caramel sauce, if you like.

To do ahead: Make the caramel sauce up to 2 days ahead and refrigerate. Cut and refrigerate the puff pastry rounds up to 1 day ahead. Cook the apples early in the day you plan to serve the tarts. Assemble the tarts and refrigerate for up to 6 hours before baking. Bake the tarts up to 1 hour before serving.

caramelized-apple walkabouts: I confess to eating two of these for breakfast. Walkabouts are turnovers: handheld triangles of delicate, flaky puff pastry wrapped around big chunks of caramelized apples. Being self-contained and portable, they're terrific for grabbing on the go, yet elegant enough for a dessert plate, served with a side of cinnamon-flavored whipped cream.

These turnovers are simple to make and a great do-ahead. Once the apples are caramelized and folded into the squares of dough, the triangles can be refrigerated overnight. Just pop them in the oven the next morning for a hot treat that will make you wish breakfast lasted all day.

Follow the directions for the preceding recipe. Cut the puff pastry into 8 squares but do not round the corners. Place 4 cooled apple quarters on one side of each square of dough. Lightly brush the edges of the square with the egg mixture. Fold the dough over so 2 opposite corners meet to form a triangle. Using the tines of a fork, seal the dough by pressing along the edges. Brush the tops of the turnovers lightly with the egg mixture and sprinkle with the 2 tablespoons sugar. Place the turnovers at least 2 inches apart on an ungreased heavy baking sheet. Bake for 30 minutes, or until golden brown. Place the baking sheet on a wire rack to cool slightly.

To do ahead: Assemble and refrigerate the turnovers, covered in plastic wrap, up to 1 day ahead. Don't bake them on the baking sheet used to refrigerate them. The cold metal will prevent the puff pastry from rising properly. (This applies to any chilled puff pastry item.) Once the oven is preheated, transfer the turnovers to another baking sheet. Brush with egg wash, sprinkle with sugar, and get them right into the oven.

caramel-roasted strawberry shortcakes

Caramelized sugar adds depth and flavor to a classic American favorite: strawberry shortcake. Here, the biscuits are heavily sprinkled with sugar, which partially caramelizes in the oven, giving them a crispy, crunchy top. The berries are oven-roasted in caramelized sugar, their red juices mixing with the golden syrup to form a beautiful caramel-flavored strawberry sauce.

The contrast of the warm shortcakes and fruit with the cool whipped cream is one of the pleasures of this dessert. Fortunately, it's easy to make the components ahead. Bake the shortcakes during dinner, reheat the strawberry caramel sauce, and assemble the dessert at the last minute.

For a stunning garnish, use Fresh Fruit in Amber Candy Coating (page 38), with stawberries, and place one on each plate.

Serves 6

Sugar-Crusted Shortcake Squares
2 cups all-purpose flour
2¹/₂ teaspoons baking powder
2 tablespoons plus 1¹/₂ teaspoons sugar
¹/₂ teaspoon salt
Pinch of grated nutmeg
Grated zest of 1 orange
¹/₂ cup (1 stick) cold unsalted butter,
**   cut into ¹/₂-inch cubes**
³/₄ cup cold whole milk, plus more for brushing

Vanilla Whipped Cream
1 cup heavy cream
1 cup crème fraîche
¹/₄ cup sugar
1 teaspoon pure vanilla extract

Caramel-Roasted Strawberries
1 cup plus 2 tablespoons sugar
¹/₄ cup water
¹/₂ teaspoon fresh lemon juice
1¹/₂ quarts (6 cups) firm, ripe strawberries, hulled
Several fresh basil leaves, sliced (optional)
1 teaspoon pure vanilla extract

6 small fresh strawberries or Fresh Fruit in Amber
**   Candy Coating using six large strawberries**
6 small basil leaves (optional)

To make the shortcake dough: In a food processor, combine the flour, baking powder, 2 tablespoons sugar, the salt, nutmeg, and orange zest. Pulse to mix. Add the butter and pulse until the mixture resembles a coarse meal with particles the size of peas and lentils. Drizzle the milk evenly over the dry ingredients and pulse a few times, just until the dough forms small clumps. Turn the dough onto a lightly floured work surface and lightly knead once or twice to form it into a mass. Gently pat or roll the dough into a 6-by-9-inch rectangle. Using a sharp knife, cut the dough into six 3-inch squares. Cover and refrigerate for up to 4 hours.

To make the whipped cream: In a deep bowl, combine all the ingredients. Whisk or beat until soft peaks form. Refrigerate until ready to serve.

To make the strawberries: Preheat the oven to 375°F. In a heavy 12-inch ovenproof skillet, gently stir the sugar, water, and lemon juice together. Using a wet pastry brush, wash down the sides of the pan.

(continued)

Bring the mixture to a boil over medium-high heat and cook, undistributed, until the sugar starts to color around the edges. Gently swirl the pan to even out the color and continue to cook until it turns a light amber. Immediately remove the skillet from the heat.

Add the strawberries and toss to coat with the caramel. Add the herb, if you're using it. Put the skillet in the oven and bake 2 or 3 minutes for small berries and up to 7 or 8 minutes for very large ones, or until the berries can be pierced with a fork but have not begun to lose their shape. Watch carefully and use a large spoon to turn large berries about halfway through baking so they are evenly basted. Remove them from the oven. It's better to slightly undercook rather than overcook the berries.

Using a slotted spoon to transfer the berries to a sieve set over a bowl; drain. Add the reserved liquid to the caramel-strawberry syrup in the skillet. Stir in the vanilla. Reserve the liquid until ready to assemble the shortcakes.

No more than 30 minutes before serving, remove the shortcake squares from the refrigerator. Lightly brush the tops with milk and sprinkle liberally with the 1 1/2 teaspoons sugar. Transfer the squares to an ungreased heavy baking sheet. Position them at least 2 inches apart if you like crusty edges or touching if you prefer soft, tender edges. Bake for 12 to 15 minutes, or until the tops are golden. Whisk the whipped cream several strokes until almost stiff.

Slit the shortcakes in half and place each bottom on a dessert plate. Spoon the berries over the shortcake bottoms and mound with a large dollop of whipped cream. Drizzle the strawberry-caramel sauce over the cream. Perch the shortcake tops at an angle like a clamshell; garnish the tops with smaller dollop of cream, a small fresh strawberry, and a small basil leaf (if you used basil). Or place a large candy-coated strawberry on each plate.

To do ahead: Make the shortcake dough and refrigerate for up to 4 hours ahead. Bake the cakes just before or during dinner. The strawberries can be roasted 4 hours in advance and kept in a sieve set over a bowl. Just before serving, add the drained juice to the caramel-strawberry syrup in the skillet and reheat. Slightly underwhip the cream and refrigerate it for up to 4 hours. Just before serving, whisk it a few quick strokes to stiffen.

shortbread tart dough

Unlike pies, which are served in their baking dish, tarts are freestanding. They are baked into ring molds with removeable bottoms so the dessert can be easily transferred to a serving plate. This cookie-like dough makes the ideal crust for dessert tarts. It's tender, slightly sweet, and simple to make. Just be careful not to overbeat the butter and sugar, or allow the butter to become too soft; the dough will be difficult to work with.

The biggest bonus of this dough is the fact that it doesn't need to be blind baked. That is, you don't need to line it with aluminum foil and fill it with weights to keep the dough from slipping down the sides of the pan in the oven. Just bake the tart straight out of the freezer.

Makes pastry for one 9-inch round or square tart or one 13-by-4-inch rectangular tart

½ cups (1 stick) cold unsalted butter, cut into pieces
¼ cup sugar
¼ teaspoon salt
½ teaspoon pure vanilla extract
1 cup plus 2 tablespoons all-purpose flour

In a food processor, process the butter, sugar, salt, and vanilla together until smooth. Using a rubber spatula, scrape the bottom and sides of the bowl and process again for a few seconds. Add the flour and pulse until the dough forms small beads. Scrape down the sides of the bowl and process for a few more seconds.

Turn the dough out onto a work surface and gather it into a ball. If rolling a round tart shell, flatten the ball into a disk. If rolling a square or rectangular tart shell, form the ball into a cylinder and flatten it into a square or rectangle.

Sandwich the dough between 2 large pieces of lightly floured waxed paper. Evenly roll the dough into a shape the same size as the pan. Remove the top layer of waxed paper and flip the dough into a tart pan with a removable bottom. Peel away the other piece of waxed paper. Don't worry if the dough breaks or tears—it is easy to repair. Press the dough evenly into the bottom of the pan. Once the bottom is even, without thin or thick spots, push the excess dough up around the sides. Remove dough from any thick spots and press it onto any thin spots. Using the side of your forefinger, press along the bottom edge all around the pan to push any excess dough up the sides: you don't want thick corners. Roll the rolling pin over the top of the pan to trim off the excess dough. Using a fork, prick the dough on the bottom about 12 times. Freeze the tart shell for at least 45 minutes or up to 3 days. Cover with plastic wrap when hard.

To bake, preheat the oven to 400°F. Wait an extra 15 minutes after the oven reaches temperature to ensure that it's very hot. Bake the frozen shell until deep golden brown, about 17 minutes, or according to instructions in the recipe. Let cool on a wire rack.

Electric mixer method: The butter should be slightly soft but still firm. On low speed, mix the butter, sugar, salt, and vanilla together until blended. Do not over-mix; you don't want to incorporate air into the dough. Using a rubber spatula, scrape the bottom and sides of the bowl. Mix in the flour just until it disappears. The dough will come together in small clumps and crumbs. Gather it into a ball and proceed with rolling.

To do ahead: Roll the dough into the tart shell. Freeze until hard, at least 45 minutes or up to 3 days.

burnt-sugar lemon tart with blueberry compote

The same technique used to broil the delicately thin, brittle sugar crust on top of crème brûlée is applied to this luscious lemon tart. It's a study in contrasts of flavor and texture: The tart, creamy lemon filling is a beguiling foil for the sweet, crunchy broiled sugar topping. It's especially good with warm, barely cooked blueberries.

Turbinado sugar, sold in supermarkets as Sugar in the Raw, is ideal for creating a caramelized topping. Under intense heat, it melts and then hardens into a crisp, firm crust. White sugar will also work, but not nearly as well. If you own a propane torch (see page 12), use it. The advantage of the torch is that it won't warm the lemon filling or darken the rim of the crust as will the broiler.

To prevent a soggy bottom, pour the warm lemon filling into a warm crust. If the shell has cooled down, reheat it for a few minutes in the oven. The empty tart shell bakes at a higher temperature than does the lemon-filled tart. Don't forget to lower the oven temperature between bakes.

Makes one 9-inch tart

1 frozen 9-inch Shortbread Tart Dough shell (page 59), in a pan with a removable bottom

2 to 3 lemons
4 large eggs
4 large egg yolks
1 cup plus 2 tablespoons sugar
4 tablespoons (½ stick) unsalted butter, cut into pieces
3 tablespoons heavy cream

Blueberry Compote
4 cups fresh blueberries
¼ cup sugar
1 teaspoon fresh lemon juice

⅓ cup turbinado sugar (see note, page 95)

To bake the tart shell: Preheat the oven to 400° F. Bake the frozen shell until deep golden brown, about 17 minutes. Transfer the pan to a wire rack. Lower the oven temperature to 350°F.

Using a vegetable peeler, scrape large strips of zest from 2 lemons, being careful not include the white pith. Squeeze the lemons, adding a third lemon if needed to make ¾ cup juice. In a medium saucepan, gently whisk the eggs, egg yolks, and sugar together. Stir in the lemon zest, lemon juice, and butter.

(continued)

Cook over medium-low heat, stirring gently and constantly with a wooden spoon or spatula until the mixture begins to thicken, about 5 minutes. It will start to thicken all of a sudden—don't let it boil. Immediately remove the pan from the heat and strain through a fine-meshed sieve into a bowl. Stir in the heavy cream.

Place the warm tart shell on a baking sheet. Pour the warm lemon filling into the tart shell. Bake for 10 to 15 minutes, or until the tart is firm about 3 inches in from the center but still wobbles slightly in the center when gently shaken. Place on a wire rack and let cool completely. Refrigerate for at least 1 hour or up to 6 hours.

Meanwhile, make the compote: In a small saucepan, combine the berries, sugar, and lemon juice. Cook over medium heat, occasionally shaking the pan, just until some of the berries begin to burst, about 5 minutes. Immediately remove from the heat.

Preheat the broiler and move the oven rack as close to the heat source as possible. If any moisture has condensed on the surface of the tart, dab it carefully with a paper towel. Place the tart on a baking sheet. Or, use a propane torch.

Evenly sprinkle the turbinado sugar over the tart. Broil for about 2 minutes, or until the sugar bubbles and a few spots begin to darken. If using a torch, hold the flame slightly above the surface of the tart and keep it moving in a circular motion. Let the sugar cool until it is brittle, about 10 minutes. Slip the ring off the tart and slide a metal palette knife underneath to release it. Slide the tart onto a serving plate or cake stand. Serve within 1 hour, with the berry compote alongside.

To do ahead: Make and roll the dough. Freeze the unbaked tart shell for up to 2 days. Assemble and bake the tart up to 6 hours before serving. Broil the sugar just before serving.

෨෨

note: As the broiler melts the sugar topping, it also blackens the rim of the crust in places. Some don't mind this and even find it attractive. If, however, you want to protect the edge of the crust, cover it with aluminum foil: Cut a 12-inch round from the foil, center the tart mold on it, and wrap the edges of the round up the sides and over the top edges, just enough to cover the rim of the crust. Most cookware stores also carry curved aluminum shields that rest on the rim of a pie or tart, made expressly for this purpose.

෨෨

caramel-nocciuola tart

The Italian word for hazelnut is nocciola *(pronounced no-chi-OH-la), and* nocciuola *(pronounced no-chi-WHO-la) is a mixture of ground hazelnuts and chocolate. Here, caramel, hazelnuts, and chocolate—the fabulous flavor trio so popular in the confectionery shops of Italy's northern provinces—come together in an easy-to-make tart. Encased in a buttery shortbread crust, the soft caramel center is crowded with crunchy whole nuts and topped with a smooth, shiny chocolate glaze.*

This is a good make-ahead dessert to serve when company is coming. Freeze the unbaked crust a day or so before, then assemble and bake the tart early in the day. Sturdy and easy to transport, it's a terrific tart to take on the road. Substitute walnuts, pecans, or toasted almonds for the hazelnuts, if you prefer.

Makes one 9-inch tart

1 frozen 9-inch Shortbread Tart Dough shell (page 59), in a pan with a removable bottom

3/4 cup sugar
3 tablespoons water
1/4 teaspoon fresh lemon juice
1 1/4 cups heavy cream
1 tablespoon unsalted butter
1 teaspoon vanilla extract
1 3/4 cups hazelnuts, toasted and skinned (see page 23)
2 large eggs

Chocolate Glaze
2 ounces good-quality bittersweet chocolate, finely chopped
1/4 cup heavy cream

Lightly Sweetened Whipped Cream (page 27) for serving

Preheat the oven to 400°F. Bake the frozen tart shell for 15 to 17 minutes or until light golden brown. It will be almost—but not quite—fully baked. Transfer the tart shell to wire rack. Lower the oven temperature to 350°F.

(continued)

caramel-nocciuola tart *continued*

To make the caramel: In a medium saucepan, stir the sugar, water, and lemon juice together. Using a wet pastry brush, wash down the sides of the pan. Bring to a boil over medium-high heat and cook, undisturbed, until the sugar starts to color around the edges. Gently swirl the pan to even out the color and continue to cook the mixture until it turns a medium amber. Immediately remove the pan from the heat.

At arm's length, stir in the cream. Return the pan to the heat and bring the caramel back to a boil. Reduce the heat to low and simmer for 5 minutes. Remove from the heat. Stir in the butter and vanilla. Set aside to cool for 5 minutes.

Arrange the nuts in a single layer on the bottom of the prebaked tart shell. In a medium bowl, lightly whisk the eggs. Gradually whisk in the warm caramel. Place the tart shell on a baking sheet and pour the caramel mixture over the nuts.

Because the outer ring of hazelnuts will show when the tart is finished, reposition the nuts if necessary to fill in any gaps. Bake for 20 to 25 minutes, or until the tart is firm about 3 inches from the center but still wobbles slightly in the center when gently shaken. Place on a wire rack to cool completely.

To make the chocolate glaze: While the tart is cooling, put the finely chopped chocolate in a small bowl. In a small saucepan, bring the cream to a boil and pour over the chocolate. Let sit for a few minutes, then gently stir until smooth and uniform in color. Set aside to thicken, stirring occasionally.

Use a small offset icing or palette knife to evenly spread the chocolate over the top of the tart leaving exposed the outer ring of caramel-covered hazelnuts closest to the crust. Refrigerate for about 15 minutes to set the chocolate. If you are transporting the tart, leave the metal ring on for protection. Otherwise, remove it. Insert a metal palette knife under the crust to loosen it from the pan bottom. Slide the tart onto a serving plate. Serve the same day, with whipped cream.

To do ahead: Make and roll the dough. Freeze the unbaked tart shell up to 2 days ahead. Toast and skin the hazelnuts up to 1 week ahead. Assemble and bake the tart up to 8 hours ahead.

caramel—coconut cream pie

Envy the guy who gets this pie in his face. It looks like the quintessential cream pie: The topping is a fluffy mass of whipped cream and toasted coconut. But beneath the billowy surface is an extraordinary soft and creamy filling, made with golden caramelized sugar and coconut milk.

Unsweetened coconut milk can be found in the Asian section of the grocery store; look for brands such as Thai Kitchen or Chef's Choice. It may not say unsweetened *on the label, but if you read the small print, there will be no sugar in the ingredients. When you open the can, the solids will be separated from the liquid. Before using, pour the contents into a bowl and whisk to combine.*

Makes one 9-inch pie

Graham Cracker Crust
1¼ cups finely ground graham cracker crumbs (about 10 sheets of crackers); see note
2 tablespoons sugar
6 tablespoons unsalted butter, melted
¾ cup sweetened flaked coconut, toasted (see facing page)

Caramel—Coconut Cream Filling
1 cup sugar
¼ cup water
¼ teaspoon fresh lemon juice
One 14-ounce can unsweetened coconut milk
1 cup plus 2 tablespoons whole milk
4 large egg yolks
¼ cup cornstarch
¼ teaspoon salt
2 tablespoons unsalted butter
1 teaspoon pure vanilla extract

Whipped Cream Topping
1½ cups heavy cream
3 tablespoons confectioners' sugar
1 teaspoon pure vanilla extract

To make the crust: Preheat the oven to 375°F. In a medium bowl, stir the crumbs and sugar together. Add the melted butter and stir well. Press the crumb mixture into the bottom and up the sides of a 9-inch glass pie plate—but not up over the rim of the plate. Freeze for 15 to 20 minutes. Bake for 10 minutes, or until it begins to color. If the crust slips down a bit, don't worry—it won't affect the outcome. Sprinkle $1/4$ cup of toasted coconut over the bottom of the baked pie shell. Set aside.

To make the filling: In a medium sauce pan, stir the sugar, water, and lemon juice together. Using a wet pastry brush, wash down the sides of the pan. Bring to a boil over medium-high heat and cook, undisturbed, until the sugar starts to color around the edges. Gently swirl the pan to even out the color and continue to cook until the mixture turns a deep amber. Immediately remove the pan from the heat.

At arm's length, gradually stir in the coconut milk, it will bubble up. Stir in 1 cup milk. Bring the mixture to a boil, stirring occasionally, to dissolve any caramel on the bottom of the pot. Remove from the heat and set aside to cool for about 5 minutes.

In a medium bowl, whisk the egg yolks with the remaining 2 tablespoons milk. Sift in the cornstarch, add the salt, and whisk until smooth, scraping down the sides of the bowl with a rubber spatula, as needed.

Gradually whisk the warm caramel milk into the egg mixture. Return the liquid to the saucepan and cook over medium heat, whisking gently and constantly until it comes to a boil. Boil for 1 full minute, stirring constantly and making sure to reach the corners of the pot. It will thicken considerably. Remove from the heat and add the butter and vanilla; stir occasionally until the butter melts.

Strain the caramel cream filling into the pie shell and spread evenly. Press plastic wrap directly onto the surface. Let cool, then refrigerate until chilled, at least 3 hours.

To make the topping: No more than 2 hours before serving, in a deep bowl, beat the heavy cream, confectioners' sugar, and vanilla together until almost stiff. Mound the whipped cream over the pie and sprinkle with the remaining $1/2$ cup toasted coconut. If you're handy with a pastry bag, mound about half the whipped cream in the center of the pie and use the remaining to pipe a decorative border around it. Sprinkle inside the decorative border with a ring of toasted coconut. Serve within 2 hours.

To do ahead: Make and freeze the graham cracker crust up to 2 days ahead. Toast the coconut up to 1 day ahead. Chill the pie for up to 8 hours before adding the topping.

Toasting Coconut: Spread the coconut on a rimmed baking sheet and toast, in a preheated 300°F oven, stirring occasionally, until light golden, 7 to 10 minutes. Watch carefully: Sweetened coconut burns easily. Cover and store at room temperature.

༄

note: Use a food processor to make finely ground graham cracker crumbs or place the crackers in a self-sealing plastic bag and crush with a rolling pin.

༄

Fancy cakes, coffee cakes, and upside-down cakes

Caramel finds its way into layer cakes, coffee cakes, and upside-down cakes in both familiar and unconventional fashion.

Pineapple upside-down cake and sticky buns are two American standards that feature caramel. In both cases, brown sugar and butter blanket the bottom of the baking pan, which is topped with batter or yeast dough. In the oven, the caramel bubbles and boils, cooking to a thick burnt-sugar syrup. Inverted, the syrup oozes, soaking the cake or sweet buns below. There are a multitude of variations on this caramel upside-down theme. Along with the classic cakes, a few more, such as Caramel Peach-Bottom Babycakes and a variation on sticky buns called Caramel Breakfast Bubble Cake, are included in this section.

Caramel also finds its way into icings and fillings. Whipped cream, cream cheese frosting, and nut fillings that are conventionally flavored with white sugar have a depth and complexity that can't be matched when the sugar is replaced with caramel. Chocolate Soufflé Roulade with Caramel Whipped Cream, and Pumpkin Cake with Caramel and Cream Cheese frosting are perfect examples.

Tips for Making and Serving Layer Cakes

· Cooking spray, such as Pam, works well for greasing cake pans, as does softened butter applied with a pastry brush. Contrary to common practice, layer cakes rarely require the sides of the pan to be greased. A round of parchment paper or waxed paper adhered to the bottom of the pan with butter or spray is usually adequate.

· Many recipes for batters and doughs call for softened butter. If you have the forethought, unwrap the stick, cut it in pieces, and leave at room temperature to soften until it yields to your finger but is not overly soft or oily. If, however, you're ready to bake and the butter isn't, slice it, place it on the paper wrapping, and zap it in the microwave for a few seconds.

· The easiest way to sift dry ingredients and add them to the mixing bowl without spilling, or to add them in increments, is to combine them in a strainer over a piece of waxed paper and shake. Lift the paper and pour the dry ingredients into the mixing bowl.

· A flexible metal palette knife, also known as an icing knife or spatula knife, is a handy tool for cake baking and decorating. The tip of the blade is rounded and the blade bends for easy maneuvering. An assortment of sizes, ranging from 4- to 14-inch blades, are used for all sorts of tasks, from leveling the flour in a measuring cup to spreading the frosting on the finished cake. An offset palette knife has a blade that bends at a slight angle, making it useful for spreading and leveling the batter in a cake pan.

· Use a revolving cake decorating stand when assembling a layer cake. It enables you to view the cake from all sides and allows you to evenly spread the filling and frosting. Heavy cast-iron cake stands can be purchased at well-stocked cookware stores. Alternatively, improvise a cake stand using an inverted cake pan that you can rotate on the work surface as needed.

· It is easier to frost or glaze a cake with a smooth, even surface. To achieve this, position the final cake layer bottom-side up, so that the part that was against the pan bottom becomes the top.

· Professional bakers place a corrugated cardboard cake round under the bottom layer when assembling a cake. Among other things, this supports the cake, making it easy to maneuver when finished. Cake rounds can be purchased in cake decorating supply or cookware stores. If you can't make or buy one, assemble the cake directly on the cake stand or inverted cake pan, then slide an 8- or 10-inch palette knife underneath to release the cake from the decorating stand or inverted cake pan. Supporting it underneath with two metal spatulas, carefully transfer the cake to the serving plate.

· To serve, cut slices using a sharp 8- or 10-inch knife. Between cuts, run the knife under hot water or wipe it with a dish towel moistened with hot water. When cutting at the table in front of guests, a wet dish towel covered with cake gunk is not a pretty sight. Fold it neatly and place on a plate (to prevent it from soaking the tablecloth). Between cuts, wipe the knife off inside the folds.

chocolate—caramel crunch cake

Caramel crunch is essentially brittle with extra baking soda. When the soda is added to caramel, it erupts into a bubbling, foamy, molten mass that cools into a light, porous candy. The texture is so airy, it melts in your mouth, making it a wonderful component in a layer cake.

Here, whipped cream and caramel crunch made with hazelnuts are used as fillings between the layers of devil's food cake. Bake this cake for a birthday or special occasion: The shiny, dark chocolate glaze that blankets it is an elegant background on which to write a message.

Alkaline ingredients such as baking soda darken caramel, so cook the sugar only until it is light amber in color. You can also substitute salted dry-roasted peanuts for the hazelnuts. If you don't want to use nuts at all, omit them and double the crunch recipe.

Makes one 3-layer cake

Shiny Chocolate Ganache Glaze
10 ounces high-quality semisweet or bittersweet chocolate, finely chopped
1 cup heavy cream

Caramel Crunch
3/4 teaspoon baking soda
3/4 cup sugar
2 tablespoons water
2 tablespoons light corn syrup
1 cup hazelnuts, toasted and skinned (see page 23), or salted dry-roasted peanuts

Cream Filling
1 1/2 cups heavy cream
1 cup crème fraîche
1/4 cup sugar
1 teaspoon pure vanilla extract

The Devil's All-Purpose Chocolate Cake (page 86)

To make the glaze: Put the finely chopped chocolate in a small bowl. In a small saucepan, bring the cream to a boil and pour over the chocolate. Let sit for a minute to melt the chocolate. Gently stir with a rubber spatula until smooth and uniform in color. Set aside and let cool to room temperature, stirring occasionally, about 1 hour.

To make the crunch: Lightly butter a baking sheet or line it with parchment paper or a silicone mat. Measure the baking soda onto a small piece of waxed paper; set aside. In a medium saucepan, stir the sugar, water, and corn syrup together. Using a pastry brush, wash down the sides of the pot with water. Bring to a boil over medium-high heat and cook, undisturbed, until the sugar starts to color around the edges. Gently swirl the pan to even out the color and continue to cook until the mixture turns a light amber. Immediately remove the pan and stir in the nuts. Stir in the baking soda; it will foam. Pour the mixture onto the prepared baking sheet. Do not spread. Let cool completely.

Transfer the slab to a cutting board covered with waxed or parchment paper (to catch the crumbs) and use a sharp knife to cut into 1/2-inch pieces. (Don't use a food processor—it pulverizes the crunch.) Set aside 1 cup of the crunch for garnish.

(continued)

chocolate—caramel crunch cake *continued*

To make the filling: In a deep bowl, combine all the ingredients. Beat until it holds soft peaks. If using an electric mixer, finish whisking by hand until it holds stiff peaks.

To assemble the cake: Place one layer of cake on a revolving cake-decorating stand or an inverted 9-inch cake pan. Using a metal icing or palette knife, spread a thin layer of the whipped cream over the bottom layer of the cake. Cover the cream evenly with 1½ cups crunch. Top the crunch with a thicker layer of whipped cream, spreading it just to the edges. (Use a total of half the whipped cream on the first layer.) Top with the middle layer of cake, pressing it to level. Spread with another thin layer of cream, sprinkle with the remaining 1½ cup crunch, and spread with the remaining half of the whipped cream. Top that with the final layer of cake, bottom up. Gently press the cake to level and, rotating the cake stand, lightly scrape around the outside edge of the cake with the palette knife to even off any cream peeking out. Brush any loose crumbs off the top and sides of the cake.

Rotating the cake stand, use the metal icing or palette knife to spread a very thin layer of chocolate glaze onto the sides and top of the cake. This is an undercoat to create a smooth surface and fill in any gaps before you pour the finishing glaze; don't use more than 1 scant cup of glaze at this time. Refrigerate for 5 minutes, or until firm to the touch.

To glaze the cake, the chocolate must be cool but pourable. If necessary, warm it slightly by placing the bowl directly over low heat for a few seconds, stirring constantly. Pour all the chocolate into the center of the cake. Working quickly with just a few strokes, use a clean dry icing or palette knife to spread the glaze so that it runs evenly over the edges and down the sides. Smooth the sides as you rotate the cake, picking up any drips to patch bare spots. Do not try to respread the glaze on the top, as it will leave marks. Refrigerate the cake until 30 to 45 minutes before serving.

Slide a long palette knife underneath the cake to release it. Supporting it with 2 metal spatulas, transfer the cake to a platter or cake stand. Sprinkle the reserved cup of caramel crunch around the top outer edge of the cake; be sure to include some of the fine dust. Serve immediately.

To do ahead: If the weather is cool and dry, the caramel crunch can be made 1 day ahead and stored, uncovered, at room temperature. Otherwise, make it the day it will be served. The other components can be made a day ahead. Cover the cake layers with plastic wrap; don't refrigerate. Refrigerate the chocolate glaze. Reheat in a small saucepan over low heat for a short time, stirring constantly, or microwave it for a few seconds, just until softened. Whip the cream until soft peaks form and refrigerate for up to 3 hours. When ready to assemble the cake, whisk it until stiff peaks form.

note: For classy-looking chocolate-on-chocolate lettering, reserve about 1/4 cup of the chocolate glaze. Fill a small paper cone or pastry bag fitted with a writing tip with the chocolate and pipe a message on the finished cake.

chocolate soufflé roulade with caramel whipped cream

Lighter than air, this flourless chocolate cake roll, filled with caramel whipped cream, literally melts in your mouth. One of my favorite desserts to serve to company, it's simple, elegant, and easy to make.

To make the filling, heavy cream is stirred into hot caramel; it's chilled, then whipped. Make it in advance to allow time for the cream to cool before beating.

This log-shaped cake requires a serving platter about 17 inches long and at least 5 inches wide. A wooden bread board or marble cheese slab works well. Or, stack and tape together a few long cardboard rectangles and cover with gold foil and/or doilies.

Makes one 17-inch-long cake roll

Caramel Whipped Cream
1¼ cups sugar
5 tablespoons water
¼ teaspoon fresh lemon juice
2½ cups heavy cream
1 teaspoon pure vanilla extract
½ teaspoon instant coffee granules

Chocolate Soufflé Roulade
4 ounces high-quality semisweet or
    bittersweet chocolate, chopped
8 large eggs at room temperature
1⅓ cups sugar
¼ teaspoon salt

1½ cups fresh raspberries
Gold Dust and Nuggets (page 137), optional

To caramelize the sugar: In a medium saucepan, gently stir the sugar, water, and lemon juice together. Using a wet pastry brush, wash down the sides of the pan. Bring to a boil over medium-high heat and cook, undisturbed, occasionally washing down the sides of the pan, until the sugar starts to color around the edges. Gently swirl the pot to even out the color and continue to cook the mixture until it turns a dark amber. Immediately remove from heat.

At arm's length, gradually stir in the cream; it will bubble up. Return the pan to the heat and stir just until the cream begins to boil. Remove the mixture from the heat; strain the mixture into a heatproof container. Add the vanilla extract. This is the base for the caramel whipped cream.

Let cool. Refrigerate until cold, at least 3 hours or as long as overnight.

To make the roulade: Preheat the oven to 325°F. Melt the chocolate and set aside (see page 117.) Spray or butter the bottom and sides of a 17-by-12-inch rimmed baking sheet. (This is known in the professional kitchen as a *half sheet pan.* Formerly available only in restaurant supply stores, it can now be purchased in most well-stocked cookware shops.) Line the baking sheet with parchment paper so that it overhangs the edges, pressing it into the corners.

Separate the eggs into 2 large bowls. Using an electric mixer (fitted with the whip attachment, if you have a choice), beat the egg yolks on medium-high speed for 1 minute. Gradually add 2/3 cup sugar and beat for about 4 minutes on medium-high speed until fluffy and quite thick. Using a rubber spatula, fold in the melted chocolate. Set aside. Wash the beaters with soap and warm water; dry thoroughly. (When beating egg whites, it is essential that all utensils be free of grease. Just to be sure, I like to wipe the bowl, whip, and rubber spatula with a little white vinegar before using.) Beat the whites on medium-high speed until they become foamy. Add the salt and beat until soft peaks form. Gradually beat in the remaining 2/3 cup sugar, a few teaspoons at a time, until all the sugar is added and stiff, glossy peaks form. Using the rubber spatula, stir one-fourth of the meringue into the chocolate mixture to lighten it. Carefully fold the remaining meringue into the chocolate mixture in 2 additions. Pour the batter into the prepared baking pan. Spread gently and evenly with an icing or palette knife, being careful not to deflate the mixture. Bake for 30 minutes. Place the baking sheet on a wire rack to cool completely.

To assemble the roulade: Place a dish towel on the table and invert the roulade onto it, positioning it so that the longer sides are on the top and bottom. Lift off the pan and carefully peel off the parchment paper.

To finish the whipped cream: Add the coffee granules and beat the caramel cream until it holds soft peaks; finish whisking by hand until it holds stiff peaks. Reserve a scant 2 cups of the cream to decorate the top. Using an icing or palette knife, spread the remaining cream evenly over the surface of the cake, leaving a 1/2-inch border along the top edge. Scatter about 1 cup raspberries over the surface. Starting at the bottom edge, lift the towel to start rolling up the cake. Once the bottom edge is tucked under, continue to roll it, using the towel as necessary to nudge it over. Remove the towel.

Using a serrated knife, cut about 1/2 inch from each end of the roll. Place the serving platter next to the cake. Roll the cake onto the platter or, supporting it underneath with metal spatulas, lift it onto the platter, seam-side down. Fit a large pastry bag with a number 5 star tip; fill with the reserved whipped cream. Pipe a decorative design along the spine of the roulade (pipe large linked stars or swirls) and garnish with the remaining fresh raspberries placed at even intervals. Serve immediately or refrigerate for up to 4 hours. Just before serving, sprinkle with Gold Dust and Nuggets, if you like. Slice with a serrated knife, wiping the knife off with a warm, wet dish towel between cuts.

To do ahead: Make the Caramel Whipped Cream 1 day ahead, but don't beat it until ready to assemble the cake.

caramel peach-bottom babycakes

This is one of my personal favorites; it reminds me of the syrup-soaked cornbread my Southern-born mother used to make. Individual yellow cornmeal cakes are topped with luscious caramel-roasted peach halves. They're baked upside down. When inverted, the caramel soaks the cake around the soft peach, but the edges of the cake stay crunchy. A beautiful contrast in textures and tastes.

I prefer to bake these in small ceramic bowls that resemble deep coffee cups without handles, but Pyrex cups or ceramic ramekins also work well.

Makes 6 individual cakes

Caramel-Roasted Peaches
1/2 cup sugar
2 tablespoons water
1/4 teaspoon fresh lemon juice
3 large, ripe but firm peaches, halved and pitted
2 tablespoons unsalted butter
1/2 teaspoon pure vanilla extract

Midsummer Cornmeal Cake batter (page 87)
Lightly sweetened whipped cream (page 27)
  or vanilla ice cream for serving (optional)

Preheat the oven to 375°F. Use a pastry brush to lightly butter the insides of six 10-ounce ovenproof bowls, ramekins, or custard cups.

To make the caramel: In a heavy 10-inch oven-proof skillet, gently stir the sugar, water, and lemon juice together. Using a wet pastry brush, wash down the sides of the pan. Bring the mixture to a boil over medium-high heat and cook until the sugar starts to color around the edges. Gently swirl the pan to even out the color and continue to cook the mixture until it turns a light amber. Immediately remove the skillet from the heat.

Add the fruit halves, cut-sides down, and put the skillet in the oven and bake for about 5 minutes, or until the caramel darkens and the fruit begins to soften. Using a fork, turn the fruit cut-side up and bake another 3 to 6 minutes, or until it can be pierced easily with a fork. The fruit should be soft but not falling apart.

Place an oven mitt over the skillet handle to remind you it's hot. Using a slotted spoon, place the peach halves, cut-sides up, in the prepared cups. Return the skillet to the heat and whisk in the butter. Bring it to a boil and immediately remove from the heat. When the bubbles subside, whisk in the vanilla. Pour the caramel sauce over the peaches, dividing it evenly between the cups. Invert each peach half so it is cut-side down.

Reduce the oven temperature to 350°F. Scrape the cake batter into the cups, dividing it evenly. It will be stiff and seem like a scant amount. Use a small spatula to level the batter. Place the cups on a baking sheet and bake for about 25 minutes, or until a skewer inserted in the center comes out clean. Remove from the oven.

Wait 1 minute, then run a small palette knife around the edge of the cups and invert each onto one of 6 dessert plates. Lift off the cups. Use a spoon to scrape out any caramel remaining inside the cups. Serve immediately, with whipped cream or ice cream, if you like.

pear or plum upside-down cake

I would be remiss to exclude this traditional caramel dessert from a book on the subject. Normally layered with pineapple, the gooey, caramelized brown sugar bottom becomes the top of the cake when it's flipped upside-down onto a plate. Instead of the traditional butter cake, a moist marzipan-flavored cake supports the fruit in this recipe.

Slices of pear and a scattering of cranberries serve as the seasonal fruit topping in winter. For summer baking, substitute plums. Cool slightly before serving to allow time for the caramel topping and fruit juices to seep down into the cake.

Makes one 9-inch cake

Caramel Fruit Topping
3 tablespoons unsalted butter, cut into pieces
3/4 cup firmly packed light brown sugar
1/4 teaspoon ground ginger (optional)
2 large, firm but ripe Bosc pears, peeled, cored, and cut into 1/2-inch slices or 4 plums (1 1/4 pounds), pitted and cut into 1/2-inch slices
1/2 cup dried or fresh cranberries (optional)

Marzipan Cake
One 7-ounce tube almond paste (*not* marzipan)
1/2 cup (1 stick) unsalted butter, softened
1/2 cup granulated sugar
2 large eggs at room temperature
1/4 teaspoon almond extract
1 teaspoon pure vanilla extract
1 cup all-purpose flour
1 teaspoon baking powder
1/4 teaspoon salt
1/2 teaspoon ground ginger
1/4 cup milk at room temperature

Lightly Sweetened Whipped Cream (page 27)

Preheat the oven to 350°F.

To make the topping: In a small saucepan, melt the butter over low heat. Using a wooden spatula, stir in the brown sugar and the ginger, if using. Boil for 1 minute, stirring. Pour the caramel into an ungreased 9-inch cake pan. Tilt and shake the pan to coat the bottom with the caramel. (If the sugar crystallizes, don't worry. Pour the mass into the pan and spread it as best you can. When it cools, crumble it evenly over the pan bottom—the sugar will melt in the oven.) Overlap the pear slices, pointy ends toward the center, around the cake pan. Scatter the cranberries, if using, in the center and in the gaps between the pears. If using plums, overlap the slices in 2 concentric circles. Set aside.

To make the cake: In the bowl of an electric mixer, cream the almond paste, butter, and sugar on medium-high speed until light and fluffy, 4 to 5 minutes. Using a rubber spatula, scrape down the sides of the bowl as needed. Don't skimp on the time—a well-creamed mixture makes a lighter cake. Add the eggs, one at time, beating a minute or so after each is added. Add the almond and vanilla extracts. Scrape down the sides of the bowl. Sift the flour, baking powder, salt, and ginger onto a piece of waxed paper. On low speed, add the dry ingredients, alternating with the milk, just until incorporated. Don't overmix at this stage; use the spatula to stir in the last bit by hand. Spread the batter evenly over the fruit.

Bake for about 50 minutes, or until the top springs back when lightly touched. Let cool on a wire rack for exactly 5 minutes. Run a small knife around the edge of the cake to release it. Place a round, flat serving plate or cake stand over the cake pan and invert. Slowly lift off the cake pan. Let cool for 10 minutes. Serve immediately, with whipped cream.

butter cake alternative: Most people have a definite opinion on almond paste and marzipan—they either love the flavor or hate it. If you're baking for the latter sort, replace the almond paste cake with a simple, tender butter cake.

1/2 cup (1 stick) unsalted butter, softened
1 cup sugar
2 large eggs at room temperature
1 1/2 cups all-purpose flour
1 1/2 teaspoons baking powder
1/4 teaspoon salt
1/2 teaspoon ground ginger
1 teaspoon vanilla extract
1/4 teaspoon almond extract
1/2 cup milk at room temperature

The technique is the same as for the Marzipan Cake: Cream the butter and sugar until light and fluffy; gradually add the eggs. Sift the dry ingredients and add them, alternating with the milk. Bake in a preheated 350°F oven for 1 hour. Invert onto a plate, cool 10 minutes, and serve.

pumpkin cake with caramel and cream cheese frosting

Autumn has officially arrived when the spicy aroma of this cake baking in the oven drifts through the house. It is the perfect pumpkin cake: moist and dense without being heavy. Golden caramel is swirled into tangy cream cheese frosting and smeared between the layers. The top of the cake is glazed with a thick caramel that drips luxuriously down the sides. Crunchy praline pumpkin seeds, which take only moments to make, are sprinkled over the cake. Make this dessert for Libra birthdays, Halloween parties, or a Thanksgiving feast.

Makes one 10-inch Bundt cake

Caramel
1 cup sugar
1/4 cup water
1/4 teaspoon fresh lemon juice
1/2 cup heavy cream
1 teaspoon pure vanilla extract

Pumpkin Cake
3 1/3 cups all-purpose flour
2 teaspoons baking soda
1 1/2 teaspoons salt
1 tablespoon ground ginger
2 teaspoons ground cinnamon
1/2 teaspoon ground nutmeg
1/8 teaspoon ground cloves
3 cups sugar
1 cup canola oil at room temperature
4 large eggs at room temperature
One 15-ounce can pumpkin purée
2/3 cup water

Lightning Pumpkin Seed Praline
1/4 cup untoasted green pumpkin seeds
1 large egg white, lightly beaten
1 tablespoon sugar

Cream Cheese Frosting
8 ounces cream cheese (not low-fat), softened
 at room temperature
1/2 cup (1 stick) unsalted butter, softened
1/4 cup confectioners' sugar
1 teaspoon pure vanilla extract

2 tablespoons confectioners' sugar

To make the caramel: In a medium saucepan, gently stir the sugar, water, and lemon juice together. Using a wet pastry brush, wash down the sides of the pan. Bring to a boil over medium-high heat and cook, undisturbed, until the sugar starts to color around the edges. Gently swirl the pan to even out the color and continue to cook until the mixture turns a medium amber. Immediately remove the pan from the heat and, at arm's length, gradually stir in the cream. Add the vanilla and whisk to combine. Set aside to cool completely.

To make the cake: Preheat the oven to 350°F. Use a pastry brush to oil a 10-cup Bundt pan or spray it with vegetable-oil cooking spray. Sift the flour, baking soda, salt, ginger, cinnamon, nutmeg, and cloves together into a large bowl. Whisk to combine.

(continued)

In the bowl of an electric mixer on medium speed (use the whip attachment if you have a choice), beat the sugar and oil until blended. Beat in the eggs, one at time, and continue to beat until fluffy, thick, and pale in color, about 3 minutes. Blend in the pumpkin and water. By hand, gradually whisk the pumpkin mixture into the dry ingredients, using a rubber spatula to scrape the sides and bottom of the bowl. Mix only until the ingredients are blended. Scrape the batter into the prepared pan and immediately place in the oven (baking soda goes into action the moment it comes in contact with liquid).

Bake for about 65 minutes, or until a skewer inserted in the center of the cake comes out clean. Let cool on a wire rack for 30 minutes. Invert the cake onto a wire rack and let cool completely.

To make the praline: Keep the oven at 350°F. Line a baking sheet with parchment paper or a silicone mat. Place the pumpkin seeds in a bowl. In a small bowl, lightly beat the egg white with a fork until foamy. Stirring with your fingers, add just enough egg white to the seeds to moisten them. If you add too much by mistake, blot the seeds with a paper towel. Toss with the sugar. Spread them out on the prepared baking sheet. Bake for about 5 minutes, turning the seeds with a metal spatula, then bake 1 minute more, or until the sugar lying loose on the parchment paper begins to turn golden.

To make the frosting: In the bowl of an electric mixer on low speed (use the paddle attachment if you have a choice), beat the cream cheese, scraping the bottom and sides of the bowl with a rubber spatula as needed, until the mixture is smooth. Add the softened butter and mix on low speed, occasionally scraping the sides and bottom of the bowl as needed, until smooth. Add the sugar and vanilla and mix on low speed until thoroughly combined. Scrape the bowl and mix again for a few seconds.

When the cake and caramel are cool, use a long serrated knife to split the cake into 3 even layers. Place the bottom layer on a cake plate, cut-side up. Using an icing or palette knife, spread the layer with a little more than half the cream cheese frosting. Drizzle about $1/4$ cup of the cooled caramel over the frosting. Top with the middle layer of cake, spread with the remaining frosting, and drizzle with another scant $1/4$ cup of caramel. Place the top layer on the cake.

Using a small whisk or fork, vigorously beat the 2 tablespoons confectioners' sugar into the remaining $1/2$ cup caramel until blended. Carefully pour the glaze over the top of the cake. It will slowly drip down but should not completely cover the cake. Sprinkle the top of the cake with the praline pumpkin seeds; you probably won't need to use them all.

To do ahead: Make the cake 1 day ahead. Let cool, cover with plastic wrap, and store at room temperature. Frost and glaze the cake on the day it's served. If the weather is dry, the Lightning Pumpkin Seed Praline can be made up to 4 days ahead.

೧௰

note: To determine the capacity of a Bundt pan, use a measuring cup to fill the pan to the top.

೧௰

very sticky buns

The sticky goop that blankets cinnamon-flavored buns is actually a brown sugar caramel. A mixture of butter and sugar is spread on the bottom of the baking pan and rounds of coiled yeast dough are placed over it. Once the buns bake to a golden brown, the pan is inverted so that the caramel oozes off the top and down the sides of the sweet rolls.

This dough is soft and rich, full of eggs and butter. It's easy to make, but like any yeast dough, it requires time to rise. Since sticky buns are best with morning coffee, you can prepare them the day before and refrigerate the pan over-night to retard the rising. The next morning, remove them from the fridge so they can rise at room temperature for 45 minutes, then pop them in the oven for a warm, sticky treat in time for breakfast or brunch.

If you're having a crowd for breakfast, divide the dough in half and make one tray of Very Sticky Buns and one Caramel Breakfast Bubble Cake (page 85).

Makes 24 buns

Sweet Yeast Dough
3 1/2 cups unbleached all-purpose flour
2/3 cup warm (110° to 115°F) milk
1 package (1/4 ounce) active dry yeast
3 large eggs
1/4 cup granulated sugar
1 teaspoon salt
1 teaspoon pure vanilla extract
1/2 cup (1 stick) unsalted butter, softened

Cinnamon-Nut Filling
1/2 cup packed dark brown sugar
2 teaspoons ground cinnamon
1/2 cup pecan halves, lightly toasted and coarsely chopped (see page 23)
1 cup raisins or dried currants (optional)

Caramel Goop
1 cup (2 sticks) unsalted butter, softened
1 cup packed light brown sugar
2 tablespoons honey

2 cups pecan halves, lightly toasted (see page 23)
2 tablespoons unsalted butter, melted

To make the dough: Measure 3 1/2 cups of flour into a small bowl so that you don't lose count of how much is added; set aside. Pour the milk into a large mixing bowl. Gently stir in the yeast and 1/2 cup of the flour. Let sit for about 15 minutes, undisturbed, or until small bubbles form on the surface. In a small bowl, whisk the eggs, sugar, salt, and vanilla together. Add the egg mixture to the bowl along with another 1/2 cup flour and beat with a large rubber spatula or wooden spoon to mix. Continuing adding flour, 1/2 cup at a time, stirring until the dough becomes too stiff to stir. Knead in all but 1/2 cup of the remaining flour. A flexible plastic scraper comes in handy here for scraping down the bowl. The dough will be soft. Knead in 2 tablespoons of the soft butter (the butter should be the same consistency as the dough). When that is incorporated, add 2 more tablespoons. Sprinkle in the remaining flour as necessary. Repeat until all the butter is incorporated.

(continued)

Turn the dough out onto a lightly floured work surface and knead for about 5 minutes, adding an additional 1 or 2 tablespoons flour, as needed, to prevent sticking. Use the dough scraper to clean the work surface and knead the scrapings back into the dough. The dough will be soft and slightly elastic, and will spring back slowly when pressed in the center.

Place the dough in a large buttered bowl, cover with plastic wrap, and let rise in a warm (but not hot) place until doubled in volume, about 2 hours.

To make the filling: In a small bowl, combine the brown sugar, cinnamon, chopped pecans, and raisins, if using. Stir to blend.

To make the goop: In the bowl of an electric mixer, cream the butter and the brown sugar together. Add the honey and blend.

Butter two 12-cup muffin pans. Spoon about $1\frac{1}{2}$ tablespoons of the goop into each of the cups. Divide the pecan halves evenly among the cups.

Turn the dough out onto a lightly floured work surface and roll into a 24-by-11-inch rectangle. Position the dough so that the long edges are at the top and bottom. Brush the surface of the dough with the melted butter. Sprinkle the dough with the filling, leaving a $\frac{1}{2}$-inch border along the top edge. Lightly press the filling into the dough. Starting at the bottom edge, roll the dough into a long log, stretching it slightly as you roll to make it somewhat tight. Pinch it along the length to seal the seam.

Using a sharp knife, slice the log in half, then cut each section in half again. Cut each quarter into 6 pieces to make 24 rounds of dough. Place a round of dough in each muffin cup and press to flatten. Cover the muffin pans loosely with plastic wrap.

At this point, the buns can be refrigerated overnight to bake the following morning or place them in a draft-free place to rise until almost doubled in volume, 45 minutes to 1 hour. If refrigerated overnight, let rise at room temperature the next day for about 45 minutes.

While the buns are rising, preheat the oven to 350°F. Bake the buns until golden brown, 20 to 25 minutes; the caramel goop will be bubbling. Let cool for 1 minute on a wire rack. Line a baking sheet with parchment paper or waxed paper and place over a muffin pan. Using oven mitts, grasp the muffin pan and baking sheet with both hands and quickly invert. Repeat with the second muffin pan. Serve warm.

To do ahead: Form the dough into buns and place in the muffin cups lined with goop. Cover the pans with plastic wrap and freeze for up to 3 days. Defrost overnight in the refrigerator and allow to rise at room temperature.

coffee cake sticky buns: Here is a pretty way to present sticky buns for company. The buns are larger than those baked in muffin pans, and they take a little longer to bake.

Spread the goop in the bottom of two 9-inch round cake pans. Scatter the pecan halves evenly over the goop. Once the dough is filled and rolled, slice the log in half, then cut each half in half again. Cut each quarter into 5 even pieces to get twenty 2-inch-thick coiled rounds of dough. Starting with 3 rounds in the center, arrange 10 pieces evenly in each pan on top of the goop. Let rise and bake for about 30 minutes. Let cool for 1 minute, then invert onto 2 round serving plates.

caramel breakfast bubble cake: If picking at food is your pleasure, this is the ideal coffee cake. It's composed of separate balls of dough that puff and bake into a round, lumpy-looking cake. To eat, pluck off a soft, fluffy, caramel-coated bite-sized piece. As with sticky buns, the caramel is baked in the bottom of the pan. When inverted, the round is crowned with a sticky golden coating. This is a good breakfast treat for those who don't eat nuts.

Butter two 8-inch round cake pans. Follow the master recipe for the dough, omitting the Cinnamon-Nut Filling and pecan halves. Make the goop using the same ingredients as above, but stir the brown sugar and honey into *melted* butter. Whisk to combine; don't worry if the butter separates a little. Once the dough rises, turn it out onto the work surface.

Cut the dough into 2-inch pieces and loosely shape them by rolling each piece into a 1 1/2-inch ball. Immerse each ball into the liquid goop and place in the prepared cake pans, alternating pans so that there is an equal amount of balls, about 25, in each. Pour the remaining goop over the top of the balls. Cover and let rise for about 45 minutes, or until almost doubled in volume. Bake for 30 minutes, or until the dough is golden brown; the goop will be bubbling. Wait for 1 minute, then invert each pan onto a serving plate.

quickie stickies: For almost-instant sticky buns, combine the goop with store-bought cinnamon-roll dough. Prerolled, presliced dough is packaged in a 17-ounce tube and sold in the dairy section of super-markets.

Make 1/2 recipe of the goop, spread it on the bottom of a 9-inch round cake pan, and sprinkle with 1 cup toasted pecan halves. Arrange the coiled sections of dough from the package over the goop and pecans. Bake according to the instructions on the tube, Invert onto a plate.

the devil's all-purpose chocolate cake

This is a tender, moist, all-purpose, no-fail chocolate cake. Keep it in your repertoire—it's a winner. The crumb has a slightly red tint typical of devil's food cakes. The color is due to the reaction between cocoa, which is acidic, and baking soda, which is alkaline. Be sure the unsweetened cocoa you use does not say "Dutch processed" or "alkalized" on the package, indicating that the acid has been neutralized. It makes for a smooth-tasting mellow chocolate, but it will not react properly in a recipe where baking soda is the predominant leavening. Brands commonly found in supermarkets, such as Hershey's and Ghirardelli, will work fine.

Professional bakers prefer to bake one tall layer cake, which is then sliced into thinner horizontal layers when the cake is assembled; it takes up less room in the oven. If that is your preference, pour the batter into a 9-by-2-inch cake pan and bake for about 45 minutes. Here, the batter is divided among 3 cake pans to make a triple-layer cake. It can also be divided between 2 pans or poured into about 16 muffin cups to make cupcakes. This recipe is the perfect base for the Chocolate-Caramel Crunch Cake (page 71).

Makes three 9-inch layers

¹⁄₂ cup cocoa powder (not Dutch processed)
¹⁄₂ cup boiling water
¹⁄₂ cup milk
1 ¹⁄₂ cups cake flour
1 teaspoon baking soda
¹⁄₂ teaspoon baking powder
¹⁄₂ teaspoon salt
¹⁄₂ cup (1 stick) unsalted butter, softened
1¹⁄₃ cups sugar
2 large eggs at room temperature
1 teaspoon pure vanilla extract

Preheat the oven to 350°F. Spray or butter three 9-inch round cake pans and line the bottoms with rounds of parchment paper or waxed paper.

Put the cocoa in a small bowl. Add the boiling water and stir until smooth. Add the milk; set aside. Sift the flour, baking soda, baking powder, and salt together onto a large piece of waxed paper. Using an electric mixer, beat the butter and sugar together on medium speed until pale and fluffy, 2 to 3 minutes. Add the eggs, one at a time, beating after each, scraping the bottom and sides of the bowl with a rubber spatula. Add the vanilla and beat the mixture on medium-high speed for 2 minutes.

On low speed, add the dry ingredients to the butter mixture in 3 parts, alternating with the cocoa liquid, mixing just until incorporated. Scrape the sides and bottom of the bowl with a rubber spatula and mix again for a few seconds.

Pour the batter into the prepared pans, dividing it evenly and leveling the batter with a spatula. Bake for 15 minutes, or until the tops spring back when lightly touched. Let cool on a wire rack for 15 minutes. Invert onto the rack, peel off the paper round, and let cool completely before assembling and frosting.

To do ahead: Cool the cake completely, cover in plastic wrap, and refrigerate for up to 3 days.

midsummer cornmeal cake

This is a delicious, light, easy-to-make summer cake. It's bright yellow, with a slightly crunchy exterior and tender insides. Serve the cake warm, with Caramel-Roasted Stone Fruit (page 30), Caramel-Roasted Strawberries (page 57), or Caramel-Sautéed Fruit (page 42), if you like.

Makes one 8-inch cake

6 tablespoons (3/4 stick) unsalted butter
1/2 cup yellow cornmeal, preferably stone-ground
1/2 cup plus 2 tablespoons all-purpose flour
1/3 cup sugar
3/4 teaspoon baking powder
1/4 teaspoon baking soda
1/4 teaspoon salt
3/4 cup crème fraîche
1 large egg
1 large egg yolk
1 teaspoon pure vanilla extract
Caramel-Roasted fruit (see headnote)
Lightly Sweetened Whipped Cream (page 27) or
  ice cream for serving (optional)

Preheat the oven to 350°F. Spray or butter the bottom of an 8-inch round cake pan and line it with a round of parchment paper.

Melt the butter; set aside to cool. In a medium bowl, whisk the cornmeal, flour, sugar, baking powder, baking soda, and salt together. In another bowl, combine the melted butter and crème fraîche, then whisk in the egg, egg yolk, and vanilla. Using a rubber spatula, fold the wet ingredients into the dry ingredients.

Scrape the batter into the prepared cake pan, smooth it to level, and bake for about 30 minutes, or until a skewer inserted in the center comes out clean. Let cool on a wire rack for about 10 minutes, then unmold. Serve warm, with fruit and whipped cream, if you like.

To do ahead: This cake is best served warm or within 1 hour of baking.

Custards, puddings, and mousse

Most of the creamy desserts in this section are based on custard—a mixture of sugar, eggs, and cream and/or milk. The mild flavor and soft texture of custard marry beautifully with caramel.

Two internationally renowned desserts illustrate totally different ways in which caramel enhances custard: Crème brûlée is a rich custard topped with a broiled, caramelized sugar crust. Crème caramel (or flan) is custard baked in a ramekin lined with caramelized sugar; when inverted the caramel runs down the sides in a thin golden sauce.

Caramel can also be used in less conventional ways with classic custard desserts. Crème anglaise (or English cream) is a custard dessert sauce that's gently cooked on the stove. (Chilled, churned, and flavored, crème anglaise is the base for rich, premium ice cream.) Here, the custard sauce for Meringue Snowballs is sweetened with caramelized sugar. Bread pudding is a simple dessert made by baking sliced loaves soaked in custard. In this version, the pan is lined with caramelized sugar. Inverted, it tops the dessert with a gleaming golden crown of caramel.

The texture of custard depends on the balance of ingredients. A combination of egg yolks and heavy cream makes the softest, richest custard. Whole eggs and milk, with their higher protein content, yield a leaner, firmer custard.

Tips for Making Custards

• The cream or milk is usually heated first. This allows the vanilla bean to steep in the hot liquid, infusing it with flavor. Also, heating the liquid shortens the time it takes for the custard to cook.

• If eggs (which serve to thicken and set the custard) are added all at once to hot liquid, they will cook and scramble, making the custard lumpy. To prevent this, eggs must be "tempered" before they are added to hot cream or milk. After the sugar is beaten with the eggs, some of the hot milk is gradually beaten into the egg mixture to warm it. The tempered egg mixture is then whisked back into the hot milk.

• Even when the eggs are properly tempered, there are sometimes small yellow specks of cooked egg in the custard. For completely smooth custard, strain it after the ingredients are combined.

• Whether cooking custard on the stove or in the oven, it's important that the internal temperature never reach higher than 170°F. This is the approximate temperature at which the proteins in eggs coagulate, causing custard to curdle. Rich custards made with yolks and cream have less tendency to curdle than lean custards made with whole eggs and milk. This is because the fat in the yolks and cream interferes with the ability of the protein molecules to bond or coagulate. Nonetheless, no custard should be allowed to reach the boiling point.

• In the oven, custards are baked in a water bath, or *bain-marie*, to protect them from the intense heat that could cause them to curdle. Set the molds in a pan large enough to accommodate them without touching. Fill the pan with hot water to reach halfway up the sides of the mold(s). Lining the bottom of the pan first with a dish towel or silicone mat further insulates the custard from direct heat.

• Don't overbake custard; it continues to cook once removed from the oven. Custard is done when the edges appear set but the center quivers slightly when the mold is gently shaken. Once the custard is baked and cooled, it's usually refrigerated to set it completely; cold custard is firmer than warm custard.

crème caramel (flan)

One of the most satisfying desserts after a large, filling meal is crème caramel—a delicate, light custard that is creamy without being overly rich. The baking mold is lined with hot caramel that, when inverted, forms a lovely, thin golden syrup that puddles around the custard.

In France it's sometimes referred to as crème renversée—meaning reversed, or overturned. In Hispanic countries it's called flan, and usually contains evaporated or condensed milk.

Because flan is freestanding (as opposed to other custards that are served in their baking cups), the custard must be firm enough to hold its shape. It's made with whole eggs, rather than egg yolks only, which give it more structure. Milk, rather than heavy cream, is the predominant dairy ingredient. As custards go, crème caramel is relatively lean.

Be sure to chill crème caramel well before turning it out. Serve it on a plate large enough to catch all the caramel syrup.

༼ ༽

a word of caution: Take special care when pouring, tilting, and tipping the hot caramel in the mold. Read "Caution: Hot Caramel" (page 19).

༼ ༽

Makes 6 individual custards

Caramel
1 cup sugar
1/4 cup water
1/4 teaspoon fresh lemon juice

Vanilla Custard
2 1/2 cups whole milk
1/2 cup heavy cream
2/3 cup sugar
Pinch of salt
4 large eggs
3 large egg yolks
2 teaspoons pure vanilla extract

Preheat the oven to 325°F. Line a roasting pan or large baking dish with a dish towel. Arrange the towel so that it's flat and does not hang over the sides of the pan. Set six 1-cup (8-ounce) ovenproof ramekins or cups in the pan, making sure they don't touch.

To make the caramel: In a medium saucepan, stir the sugar, water, and lemon juice together. Using a wet pastry brush, wash down the sides of the pan. Bring to a boil over medium-high heat and cook until the sugar starts to color around the edges. Gently swirl the pan to even out the color and continue to cook the mixture until it turns a medium amber. Immediately pour the hot caramel into the bottom of the ramekins, dividing it evenly among them. Carefully tilt and turn the cups to coat the sides and bottom with the caramel. Don't worry if the coating is uneven. Set aside for the caramel to cool and harden. If the weather is dry, this can be done 1 day ahead. Don't wash the pan.

(continued)

To make the custard: In the same pan (the residual caramel will add flavor), stir the milk, cream, ⅓ cup of the sugar, and the salt together. Cook over medium heat until bubbles form around the edges of the pan. Stir again to dissolve the sugar. Set aside to cool to lukewarm.

In a medium bowl, gently whisk the remaining ⅓ cup sugar, the eggs, egg yolks, and vanilla together. You want to create as few air bubbles as possible. Gradually stir the milk into the egg mixture in a slow stream. Strain the custard into a pouring pitcher (such as a Pyrex measuring cup) and divide the liquid evenly among the prepared ramekins. Place the pan in the oven and use a teapot to fill it with very hot water to reach about halfway up the sides of the ramekins. Be careful not to splash any water into the custards. Cover the pan loosely with a piece of aluminum foil (steam must be able to escape); don't allow the foil to touch the surface of the custards.

Bake for about 40 minutes, or until the edges of the custards appear firm and the centers quiver when gently shaken. Remove the ramekins from the water bath and place on a wire rack to cool completely. Cover each with plastic wrap and refrigerate for at least 6 hours or up to 2 days.

When ready to serve, carefully run a small knife around the edge of each ramekin, angling the knife towards the cup so it doesn't tear the custard. Place a dessert plate over each and quickly invert. You may have to shake the ramekin a little to release the custard. Use a spoon to scrape out any remaining caramel.

To do ahead: Refrigerate the custards for up to 2 days. Unmold just before serving.

variation: To make 1 large crème caramel, use a 9-inch, 6- to 8-cup cake pan or soufflé dish. Follow the recipe above and bake for 70 to 75 minutes. Let cool and chill as above. To serve, shake the pan gently to release the custard. If it still sticks in places, run a small knife around the edge of the pan. Place a serving platter over the top and quickly invert. Cut into wedges to serve.

coconut crème caramel: Gently whisk one 14-ounce can unsweetened coconut milk (available in the Asian section of grocery stores) with only 1 cup of whole milk. Omit the heavy cream. The coconut milk will appear partly solid in the can but will liquefy when stirred. All the other ingredients and directions are the same. For an optional garnish, just before serving, sprinkle the center with toasted coconut.

citrus crème caramel: Add the grated zest of 2 oranges and 1 lemon to the milk mixture before heating it. Reduce the vanilla extract to 1 teaspoon. The zest is strained out when the custard is poured. To serve, scatter segments of orange, tangerine, and/or mixed berries around the base.

almond flan: Add ½ teaspoon almond extract to the heated milk. To serve, scatter orange segments, peach, plum, and/or mango slices, and/or mixed berries around the base.

coffee crème caramel: Add 4 teaspoons instant coffee granules to the heated milk mixture.

crème brûlée

This is the softest, creamiest custard imaginable, baked in a cup and topped with a thin, brittle veneer of barely burnt caramelized sugar. (Brûler means "to burn" in French.) Before taking the first bite, gently crack the hard sugar crust with the back of your spoon: It's one of the most satisfying sensations in the world of desserts.

Crème brûlée is a popular and ubiquitous restaurant dessert. It's also easy to make at home. Perhaps home cooks shy away from it because the broiled sugar topping seems tricky to make; it is not. And it adds a little drama to the end of a meal: Your guests will love to gather in the kitchen and watch you wield your propane torch.

Unlike flan, which is served freestanding and therefore requires leaner, higher-protein ingredients such as milk and whole eggs to support it, this custard is served in a cup or shallow mold. It can afford to be soft, creamy, and out-rageously rich. The ingredients are pure indulgence: heavy cream and egg yolks.

After the custard is baked, it's chilled. One of the sensuous pleasures of crème brûlée is the contrast between the soft, cool custard and thin, brittle sugar crust. There are two ways to "burn" the sugar topping: with a propane torch or a broiler. I prefer the torch. It cooks the sugar quickly without heating the custard below. Under a broiler, the sugar takes 2 to 3 minutes to caramelize, and the custard underneath heats up and softens. Custards broiled in the oven are best refrigerated again for at least 30 minutes to chill and firm—which is just about when the caramelized sugar crust will begin to melt. I suggest investing in a propane torch from the hardware store: it's cheaper and stronger than the small torches sold in fancy cookware stores. It's also terrific for browning meringues.

Makes 8 individual custards

4 cups heavy cream
2/3 cup granulated sugar
Pinch of salt
1 vanilla bean, split lengthwise
12 large egg yolks
About 1/2 cup turbinado sugar (see note)

Preheat the oven to 300°F. Line a roasting pan or large baking dish with a dish towel. Arrange the towel so that it's flat and does not hang over the sides of the pan. Set eight 3/4-cup (6-ounce) ovenproof ramekins or cups in the pan, making sure they don't touch.

In a medium saucepan, stir the cream, 1/3 cup granulated sugar, and the salt together. Using a paring knife, scrape the seeds from the vanilla bean into the cream and add the pod as well. Cook over medium heat until bubbles form around the edges of the pan. Stir again to dissolve the sugar. Set aside to cool to lukewarm.

In a medium bowl, gently whisk the remaining 1/3 cup granulated sugar and egg yolks together. You want to create as few air bubbles as possible. Remove the vanilla pod and gradually stir the cream into the egg mixture in a slow stream. Strain the custard into a pouring pitcher (such as a Pyrex measuring cup) and divide the liquid evenly among the prepared ramekins.

Place the pan in the oven and use a teapot to fill it with very hot water about halfway up the sides of the ramekins. Be careful not to splash any water into the custards.

Bake for 30 to 35 minutes, or until the edges are set and the centers quiver when gently shaken. If using shallow crème brûlée molds, they may set in as little as 25 minutes. A small knife inserted halfway between the center and the edge of the custard should come out clean or almost clean. Remove the ramekins from the water bath and transfer to a wire rack to cool completely. Cover each with plastic wrap and refrigerate until cold, at least 4 hours or up to 2 days.

Uncover the ramekins; if there is condensation on the surface of the custards, dab it with a paper towel. Scatter about 2 teaspoons turbinado sugar over the surface of each custard, tilting and shaking it to evenly distribute. Caramelize the sugar in one of the following ways.

Propane torch method: If you've never used a torch, get instructions from the hardware store where you purchase it. Make sure there is nothing flammable, such as paper, nearby. Place the custards on a baking sheet to protect the counter. Hold the torch so the flame touches the surface of the sugar. Keep it constantly moving in a circular motion until the sugar is bubbling vigorously and begins to darken in places. Let the caramelized sugar cool and harden. Serve immediately or within 30 minutes.

Broiler method: Preheat the broiler to the hottest setting and move the oven rack as close to the heat source as possible. Put the ramekins on a baking sheet and place under the broiler for about 2 minutes, or until the sugar bubbles vigorously and begins to darken in places. Leave the oven door slightly open so you can watch and turn the tray if necessary. Remove the ramekins from the baking sheet and refrigerate, uncovered, for at least 5 minutes, but no more than 30 minutes.

To do ahead: Refrigerate the custards up to 2 days ahead. Broil the sugar topping within 30 minutes of serving.

⟨෧⟩

note: Turbinado is a coarse, golden, partially refined free-flowing sugar. It's sold in supermarkets as Sugar in the Raw. White sugar also works fine as a crème brûlée topping, but turbinado is easier to spread over the surface of the custard and yields a more substantial, longer-lasting crust. Brown sugar, because of its high moisture content, must be dried first in the oven. It's hardly worth the effort.

⟨෧⟩

caramel crown bread pudding

Imagine the creamiest, fluffiest French toast you've ever tasted in the form of a cake topped with a glistening, golden caramel. Caramel bread pudding is elegant comfort food. It's a warming dessert on a winter evening or serve it for a holiday breakfast when family and friends are gathered.

Serves 6 to 8

Caramel
1¼ **cups sugar**
⅓ **cup water**
½ **teaspoon fresh lemon juice**

About half to three-fourths of a 1-pound challah
 or brioche loaf
5 **large eggs**
6 **tablespoons sugar**
1¼ **cups heavy cream**
2½ **cups whole milk**
1½ **teaspoons pure vanilla extract**
¼ **teaspoon almond extract**
¼ **cup raisins**

To make the caramel: Have ready a 9-by-2-inch round cake pan. In a medium saucepan, gently stir the sugar, water, and lemon juice together. Using a wet pastry brush, wash down the sides of the pan. Bring to a boil over medium-high heat and cook, undisturbed, until the sugar starts to color around the edges. Gently swirl the pot to even out the color and continue to cook until the mixture turns a medium amber. Immediately pour the hot caramel into the cake pan. Grasping the pan with oven mitts, carefully tilt and turn it to evenly coat the bottom and sides with the caramel. Set aside for the caramel to cool and harden. If the weather is dry, this can be done 1 day ahead.

Cut the loaf of bread in half (horizontally if it's a long loaf). Cut one section (and possibly part of the second section, depending on the size of your loaf) into 1-inch-thick slices. In a medium bowl, whisk the eggs, sugar, cream, milk, and vanilla and almond extracts together. Pour the liquid into a flat-bottomed baking dish. Soak a few slices of bread in the liquid, turning them to saturate both sides as you would with French toast. Repeat with the remaining bread, stacking the slices in the dish to make room, until all the bread is moistened.

Overlap the slices of bread in the prepared cake pan. (Whatever is facing down will be the side shown when the pudding is inverted). Sprinkle the raisins between the slices as you arrange them. Press gently to flatten. Pour any liquid remaining in the baking dish over the bread and let it sit at room temperature for 30 minutes, pushing down on it occasionally to immerse the bread.

Preheat the oven to 350°F. Set the cake pan in a large baking dish. Fill the dish with hot water to reach half-way up the sides of the cake pan. Bake for 45 minutes, or until a skewer inserted in the center of the pudding comes out clean and the custard looks set. Remove the cake pan from the water bath and let cool on a wire rack for 10 minutes. Run a small knife around the edge of the pan to loosen the pudding. Place a serving plate (or cake stand) face down over the top of the cake pan. Grasping the pan and plate with oven mitts, invert the bread pudding onto the plate. Some of the caramel will stick to the pan; it's okay—there's plenty. Serve warm.

To do ahead: Line the cake pan with caramel 1 day ahead. You can also assemble and refrigerate the bread pudding up to 8 hours before baking.

meringue snowballs in caramel crème anglaise

Oeufs à la neige, *or snow eggs, is a classic old-fashioned French dessert, still served occasionally in fine restaurants here and abroad. It's a marriage of textures: Light, airy oval scoops of meringue are set on a pool of rich, creamy custard sauce, or crème anglaise. The dish is drizzled with thin golden filaments of caramelized sugar.*

Here, the caramel theme is taken one step further: The custard sauce itself is made with caramelized sugar, giving it a luxurious golden hue and depth of flavor. The meringue is formed with an ice cream scoop, creating a snowball shape.

This dessert is sometimes called floating island, *but technically speaking, that is a baked meringue, often quite large, sitting in a puddle of custard sauce. Oeufs à la neige are poached on the stove in almost-simmering water or milk. There is economy in this dessert: The custard sauce is made using the poaching milk and the egg yolks that were separated from the whites when making the meringue.*

Serves 6

Meringue Snowballs
3 to 4 cups whole milk
6 large egg whites
Pinch of salt
³/4 cup sugar, preferably superfine
1 teaspoon pure vanilla extract

Caramel Crème Anglaise
²/3 cup plus 1 tablespoon sugar
3 tablespoons water
1 tablespoon light corn syrup
2 cups reserved milk from snowballs
1 vanilla bean, split lengthwise
1 teaspoon pure vanilla extract
6 large egg yolks

Caramel Drizzles
¹/2 cup sugar
2 tablespoons water
¹/4 teaspoon fresh lemon juice

To make the snowballs: Fill a 10-inch skillet about halfway with the milk and cook over medium heat until bubbles form around the edges. (It should steam, not boil; a thermometer will register about 185°F.) Adjust the heat to maintain the temperature; the milk should not simmer. Meanwhile, put the egg whites in a clean (grease-free), large mixing bowl and beat on medium speed. When the whites are foamy, add the salt and continue beating until soft peaks form. Gradually add the sugar, 1 tablespoon at a time, beating about 20 seconds between additions and increasing the mixer speed to medium-high, until stiff, glossy peaks form. Add the vanilla about halfway through.

Line a baking sheet with paper towels and place next to the stove. Using a 2-inch spring-loaded ice cream scoop, swipe a rounded mound of meringue from the bowl. Use a spoon to round off and smooth the top of the meringue. (Rinse the scoop and spoon under warm water occasionally to remove excess meringue.)

Drop the meringue into the hot milk. Do not allow the milk to simmer. Continue to drop balls into the liquid, leaving enough room so that they don't touch; 6 or 7 will fit in a 10-inch skillet. After 2 minutes, turn each meringue to poach the underside: Lift it with a soup spoon, turn it onto another soup spoon, then lower the meringue into the milk. Cook for another 2 minutes, then use a slotted spoon to transfer the cooked meringues to the paper-lined baking sheet. Repeat with the remaining meringue to make a total of 18 to 21 balls. Strain off and reserve 2 cups of the milk to use in the sauce.

To make the custard sauce: In a medium saucepan, gently stir the $2/3$ cup sugar, the water, and corn syrup together. Using a wet pastry brush, wash down the sides of the pan. Bring to a boil over medium-high heat and cook, undisturbed, until the sugar starts to color around the edges. Gently swirl the pan to even out the color and continue to cook the mixture until it turns a medium amber. Immediately remove from the heat.

At arm's length, stir in a little of the reserved milk; it will bubble up. Gradually stir in the remaining milk. Return the pan to the heat, bring the mixture to a boil, and remove from heat. Using a paring knife, scrape the seeds from the vanilla bean into the liquid and add the pod as well. Add the vanilla extract. Set aside to steep for 20 minutes.

In a medium bowl, whisk the egg yolks with the tablespoon of sugar for about 1 minute. Remove the vanilla pod from the milk. Whisking constantly, gradually pour the warm milk into the yolks. Return the liquid to the saucepan and cook over medium-low heat, stirring gently and constantly with a wooden spatula, until the mixture thickens slightly and coats the back of the spatula, 4 to 5 minutes. Do not let it boil; the temperature should not exceed $170°$F or it will curdle. Remove from the heat, whisk once, and strain. (If the custard does curdle, whirl the liquid briefly in a food processor or blender until smooth, then strain.) Set aside.

Serve the meringues within 6 hours of poaching. The custard sauce can be served warm or cold. Ladle about $1/3$ cup of sauce into each of 6 shallow bowls or dessert plates. Place 2 to 3 balls in each.

To make the Caramel Drizzles: Fill a bowl large enough to accomodate the bottom of a small saucepan with ice water. In the small saucepan, gently stir the sugar, water, and lemon juice together. Using a wet pastry brush, wash down the sides of the pan. Bring to a boil over medium-high heat and cook, undisturbed, until the sugar starts to color around the edges. Gently swirl the pan to even out the color and continue to cook the mixture until it turns a medium amber. Plunge the bottom of the pan into the ice water for 8 seconds to arrest the cooking and cool the caramel a little. When the caramel drips off the end of a fork in threads rather than in small droplets, use the fork to drizzle and swirl the caramel in a circular motion over each dish. If you're lucky, the caramel will spin very fine threads in addition to the thicker ones. Serve immediately.

To do ahead: The dessert can be made up to 6 hours before serving. Garnish with the Caramel Drizzles just before serving.

black-and-tan mousse parfait

Creamy, rich caramel and dark chocolate mousses are layered in parfait glasses for an elegant, simple do-ahead dessert. The sweetness of the former is in pleasing harmony with the bittersweet flavor of the latter.

Whipped cream gives mousse its characteristic lightness. Normally, gelatin is used to stabilize the airy mixture. Here, mascarpone cheese, a soft, dense, rich cream that holds its shape quite well when lightly beaten, eliminates the need for gelatin. Mascarpone originated in the northern hills of Italy. With our nationwide craze for tiramisu a decade back, mascarpone became so popular that it's now manu-factured here and is readily available in supermarkets.

Overwhipping the cream causes the texture of the mousse to be grainy and too stiff to flow smoothly into the parfait glass. To closely control the consistency of the cream, use a hand whisk or an electric mixer on low speed.

Serves 6

Caramel
1 cup sugar
¹⁄₄ cup water
¹⁄₄ teaspoon fresh lemon juice
1 cup heavy cream
1 teaspoon pure vanilla extract

Chocolate Mousse
2 ounces bittersweet or semisweet chocolate, finely chopped
¹⁄₄ cup hot caramel (see below)
¹⁄₂ teaspoon instant coffee granules dissolved in ¹⁄₂ teaspoon warm water
1 cup heavy cream
3 tablespoons unsweetened Dutch-processed cocoa powder, such as Droste

Caramel Mousse
1 cup reserved caramel at room temperature (see below)
³⁄₄ cup mascarpone cheese
³⁄₄ cup heavy cream
¹⁄₂ teaspoon instant coffee granules dissolved in ¹⁄₂ teaspoon warm water

Shaved, grated, or finely chopped semisweet chocolate for garnish

Have ready 6 small parfait glasses. (My favorites for this recipe are 8-ounce juice glasses shaped like inverted cones.)

To make the caramel: In a small saucepan, gently stir the sugar, water, and lemon juice together. Using a wet pastry brush, wash down the sides of the pan. Bring to a boil over medium-high heat and cook, undisturbed, until the sugar starts to color around the edges. Gently swirl the pan to even out the color and continue to cook until the mixture turns a medium amber. Immediately remove the pan from the heat. At arm's length, gradu-ally stir in the heavy cream; it will bubble up. When the bubbles subside, stir in the vanilla.

To make the Chocolate Mousse: Put the finely chopped chocolate in a medium bowl. Pour $1/4$ cup of the hot caramel and the dissolved coffee over the chocolate and stir with a small whisk or fork. Set aside, stirring occasionally, until the chocolate is melted, smooth, and cool to the touch.

Meanwhile, transfer 1 cup of the caramel to a bowl or plastic container and refrigerate for about 30 minutes, or just until cooled to room temperature. Check occasionally; don't let it get too cold. Set the remaining caramel aside in a small cup at room temperature to drizzle over the finished parfait. (Do not refrigerate; it can remain at room temperature overnight.)

In a medium bowl, combine the heavy cream and cocoa and whisk or beat on low speed, scraping the sides once with a rubber spatula, until the mixture thickens but is still pourable. It should mound ever so slightly when dropped off the whisk but will sink back to level in seconds. Do not overwhip. Pour about one-fourth of the cream into the melted chocolate. Using a rubber spatula, stir to lighten it. Fold the remaining cream into the chocolate. Clip the end of a pastry bag closed (it doesn't need a tip) and fill with the mousse.

Remove the clip and carefully pipe chocolate mousse, between the glasses, dividing it evenly. (Alternatively, carefully spoon the mousse into the glass.) Shake gently to level the mousse.

To make the Caramel Mousse: When the 1 cup caramel has cooled to room temperature, put the mascarpone and heavy cream in a medium bowl. Add the caramel and the dissolved coffee. Whisk until thickened but still pourable. It will mound ever so slightly when dropped off the whisk but will sink back to level in seconds. Do not overwhip. Carefully pour caramel mousse into a glass to cover the chocolate (the chocolate mousse will be set by now). Gently shake the glass to level the mousse. Repeat with the remaining glasses until all the mousse is used.

Refrigerate for at least 3 hours or as long as overnight. Before serving, spoon the remaining caramel over each parfait, dividing it evenly. Tilt each glass so that the caramel runs to the edges, covering the surface of the mousse. Sprinkle with chocolate.

To do ahead: The parfaits can be made and refrigerated 1 day ahead.

Cookies and bars

Caramelized sugar adds flavor and crunch to cookies. In some recipes, such as Hazelnut Praline Biscotti and Golden Stained-Glass Sugar Cookies, the caramel is made on the stove and is incorporated into cookies in the form of nut praline or amber-colored "glass." In cookies such as Palmiers and Praline Lace Cookies, it is the heat of the oven that gives the sugar its golden hue and crisp texture.

Tips on Baking Cookies with Caramelized Sugar

· A heavy, rimless aluminum baking sheet gives the best results when baking almost any cookie. To prevent the melted sugar from burning on the baking sheet, butter or line it with a piece of parchment paper, according to the recipe.

· Toward the end of the baking time, keep an eye on the color of the cookies. In a hot oven, caramelized sugar can darken and burn quickly.

· A minute or so after the cookies are removed from the oven, slide an icing or palette knife underneath to release them from the baking sheet and prevent them from sticking once the caramelized sugar hardens.

· Let the cookies cool completely before you serve them. Fresh from the oven, hot caramel burns the tongue. Warm caramel sticks in your teeth—not a pleasant sensation. Unlike some cookies that taste best warm off the baking sheet, cookies baked with caramel or caramelized sugar must cool to room temperature in order to be brittle and crunchy, the way they should be.

· Don't plan on storing these cookies for any length of time if the weather is humid. Moisture will cause any cookie to become soggy, but this is especially true of cookies that contain caramelized sugar. Store at room temperature, covered with aluminum foil.

praline lace cookies

*These delicate, crunchy caramel-flavored confections teeter
on the cusp of cookie and candy. Brown sugar caramel is
cooked stove top, thickened into a dough with finely ground
nuts and a little flour, then baked in the oven where it
spreads into perfectly flat rounds. When cool, the backs can
be painted with tempered chocolate, which peeks through
the holes of these lacy cookies.*

*Aside from the taste and texture, the most marvelous
thing about these cookies is that they're flexible: literally.
While still warm from the oven, the cookies can be shaped
into fluted dessert bowls (that make lovely ice cream sundae
dishes) or cigarette-shaped cylinders to dip in chocolate.
Pecan pieces, toasted hazelnuts, or even peanuts can be
substituted for the almonds.*

Makes 3 dozen cookies

- ½ cup plus 2 tablespoons sliced almonds
  (untoasted) or nut of your choice
- ¼ cup all-purpose flour
- 4 tablespoons (½ stick) unsalted butter,
  cut into pieces
- ¼ cup packed light brown sugar
- ¼ cup light corn syrup
- 8 ounces semisweet or milk chocolate, tempered
  (see page 118), optional

In a food processor, combine the nuts and flour and
pulse until the mixture is powdery and uniformly finely
ground. Transfer to a small bowl. In a small saucepan,
stir the butter, brown sugar, and corn syrup together.
Heat the mixture over low heat until the butter melts.
Increase the heat to high and bring the mixture to a
boil. Remove from the heat and stir the hot liquid into
the nut mixture. Let cool for at least 30 minutes; it will
thicken into a dough. Bake immediately or store the
dough, covered, in the refrigerator for up to 1 day.

Preheat the oven to 350°F. Lightly butter a heavy,
rimless baking sheet. With moistened hands, mold
rounded teaspoons of dough into balls and place them
on the baking sheet at least 3 inches apart. Arrange
no more than 9 small balls on a baking sheet; they
spread considerably. Once they spread, they will bubble
furiously in the oven. Bake for about 10 minutes, or
until the active bubbling subsides. Remove from the
oven and place the baking sheet on a wire rack. When
the cookies are firm enough to lift, after a minute or
so, use a metal spatula to transfer them to a wire rack.
Let cool completely. Repeat to bake the remaining dough.

Use a dry pastry brush to paint the backs of the cookies
with tempered chocolate, if you like. Place each cookie
chocolate-side up on a baking sheet lined with aluminum
foil, waxed paper, or parchment paper. Refrigerate until
the chocolate sets, about 5 minutes.

To do ahead: The dough can be covered with plastic
wrap and refrigerated for up to 1 day.

cigarette cookies: Follow the baking instructions for the preceding cookies. Remove from oven and place the baking sheet on a wire rack. When the cookies are firm enough to lift but are still flexible, roll one around a chopstick or the handle of a wooden spoon to form a tight cylinder, then slip the rolled cookie off the handle. Repeat with the remaining cookies. Work quickly to roll the cookies before they become cool and brittle. If the cookies become too brittle to shape, return the baking sheet to the oven for a minute or so to rewarm them. Let cool, then dip each cookie end into the tempered chocolate and place on a baking sheet lined with aluminum foil, waxed paper, or parchment paper. When the level of the chocolate gets too low to dip, use a dry pastry brush to paint the ends with chocolate. Refrigerate until the chocolate sets, about 5 minutes.

fluted dessert bowls: Have ready 3 small soup bowls measuring $4\frac{1}{2}$ to 5 inches across the top. With moistened hands, mold rounded tablespoons of dough into balls and place on the prepared baking sheet at least 7 inches apart. You can fit no more than 3 large balls on a cookie sheet; they spread considerably. Bake the cookies for about 12 minutes or until the active bubbling subsides. Remove from the oven and place the baking sheet on a wire rack. When the cookies are firm enough to lift but are still flexible, use a metal spatula to lift them, one at a time, and place in one of the soup bowls. Gently press the bottom to flatten. The sides will ruffle prettily. Repeat with the other 2 cookies. If the cookies become too brittle to shape, rewarm the baking sheet in the oven for a minute or so. Remove the cooled cookies from the bowls. Repeat to bake and form the remaining dough. If you like, use a dry pastry brush to paint the fluted rim with a thin decorative band of chocolate (using about 4 ounces of tempered chocolate). Makes 9 bowls.

note: If reusing the same baking sheet, simply wipe off the excess butter with a paper towel between batches; it's not necessary to regrease it. Be sure to let the pan cool before baking the next batch of dough.

hazelnut praline biscotti

In Italian, bis *means "twice,"* cotti *means "cooked." Biscotti are traditionally made with hazelnuts or almonds and scented with a hint of anise. Here, hazelnut praline is tossed into the dough for a caramelized-sugar spin on these crunchy, easy-to-make twice-baked cookies.*

Praline, made by stirring whole nuts into molten amber caramel, hardens into a clear, golden candy. In the oven, the sugar melts into chewy veins of caramel that run throughout the cookies. Be careful not to cook the sugar past a light amber, as the praline will continue to cook and darken in the oven.

I confess: I'm not a big fan of aniseed. But a small amount of this aromatic spice heightens the flavor of the hazelnuts. Crushing the seeds releases their flavor. Use a mortar and pestle or break them with the flat side of a chef's knife.

Makes about 2½ dozen cookies

Hazelnut Praline
½ cup plus 2 tablespoons sugar
¼ cup water
¼ teaspoon fresh lemon juice
1¼ cups hazelnuts, toasted and skinned
  (see page 23)

1¾ cups all-purpose flour
1 cup sugar
1 teaspoon baking powder
¼ teaspoon salt
¾ teaspoon aniseed, crushed (see headnote)
4 tablespoons (½ stick) cold unsalted butter,
  cut into ½-inch cubes
2 large eggs
1 teaspoon vanilla extract

To make the praline: Lightly butter a baking sheet or line it with parchment paper or a silicone mat. In a small, heavy saucepan, stir the sugar, water, and lemon juice together. Using a wet pastry brush, wash down the sides of the pan. Bring to a boil over medium-high heat and cook, undisturbed, until the sugar starts to color around the edges. Gently swirl the pan to even out the color and continue to cook until the mixture turns a medium amber. Immediately remove the pan from the heat.

Stir in the toasted hazelnuts and quickly pour the mixture onto the prepared baking sheet. Use a wooden spatula to press the praline so that it's no more than 1 nut deep. Let cool completely. When the praline is cool, use a large sharp knife to cut it into nut-sized pieces.

Preheat the oven to 350°F. Line a heavy baking sheet with parchment paper or aluminum foil.

In a food processor, combine the flour, sugar, baking powder, salt, and aniseed. Process for a few seconds to blend. Add the butter and pulse just until the butter pieces are the size of lentils. In a small bowl, lightly beat the eggs and vanilla together. Pour them evenly over the dry ingredients. Pulse a few times to blend. The mixture will appear dry and crumbly. Using a rubber spatula, scrape the bottom of the bowl, then pulse for a few more seconds.

Turn the dough out into a bowl and toss in the praline. Turn it out onto a work surface. Squeeze and mash the dough into a disk. Using a sharp knife, cut the dough in half (or use a kitchen scale to evenly divide it). Form each piece into a 12-inch log by rolling and squeezing the dough with your hands. Place the logs on the prepared baking sheet at least 6 inches apart; they will spread in the oven. Square off the ends of each log with your hands; make sure that the logs are even and no more than 12 inches long.

Bake for 25 to 30 minutes, or until the logs are golden. Remove from the oven, leaving the oven on. Immediately slide a palette knife under the logs to prevent the burnt sugar from sticking. Set aside to cool slightly on the baking sheet, 5 to 10 minutes.

Using a large sharp knife and a quick downward motion, cut each log on a slight diagonal into $1/2$-inch-thick slices. If any slices break, just press them back together—the sugar will adhere them. Lay the cookies on their sides on the baking sheet; it's okay if they're crowded. Bake for about 7 minutes, or until the undersides of the cookies show the barest hint of color. Don't overbake. Let cool for a few minutes, then slide a metal palette knife underneath the cookies to prevent them from sticking. Leave them on the sheet until completely cool; they will become firm and crunchy. Store in an airtight container at room temperature for up to 4 days.

To do ahead: If the weather is dry, make the Hazelnut Praline up to 3 days ahead. The cookies can be made up to 4 days ahead.

෧෨

note: If you don't own a food processor, you can make this dough by hand in the same way you'd make pie dough: Whisk the dry ingredients together in a bowl, cut in the butter using a pastry blender, fold in the wet ingredients, and toss in the praline. Gather the dough together, shape, and bake.

෧෨

golden stained-glass sugar cookies

As an edible ornament for the holidays, stained-glass cookies can be hung on the tree or strung across a window. Crisp sugar cookies frame translucent amber-colored "glass," made with caramelized sugar.

Normally, these cookies are made with crushed Lifesavers or lollipops. You can use the method below to do just that. But here, you make your own hard candy. Kids can help pile the cookie's open spaces with the pulverized candy, which will melt and harden into clear golden windows.

To form the cookie dough frames that surround the "glass," cut the dough using large cookie cutters. Hearts, stars, and circles all work well. Cut out openings in the center of the shapes using smaller cookie cutters.

These sugar cookies are crisp, sweet, and sturdy, with a mild buttery flavor. The dough is easy to handle; it's not too soft or sticky. The cookie edges turn lightly golden when they're fully baked. Add this recipe to your repertoire to use whenever you want to make cut-out decorated cookies— with or without stained-glass centers.

Makes 2 to 3 dozen cookies in assorted sizes

Sweet Amber Glass
1 cup granulated sugar
1/4 cup water
1/4 teaspoon fresh lemon juice

Sugar Cookies
1 3/4 cups plus 2 tablespoons all-purpose flour
1/2 teaspoon baking powder
1/4 teaspoon salt
1/2 cup (1 stick) unsalted butter, softened
2/3 cup granulated sugar
1 large egg at room temperature
1 teaspoon pure vanilla extract

1/4 cup turbinado sugar (see page 95), optional

To make the Sweet Amber Glass: Line a heavy baking sheet with parchment paper, aluminum foil, or a silicone mat. In a small saucepan, gently stir the sugar, water, and lemon juice together. Using a wet pastry brush, wash down the sides of the pan. Bring to a boil over medium-high heat and cook, undisturbed, until the sugar starts to color around the edges. Gently swirl the pan to even out the color and continue to cook the mixture until it turns a light amber. Immediately pour the molten sugar onto the prepared baking sheet. Let cool completely. Pulverize the candy by placing it in a self-sealing plastic bag and crushing it with a rolling pin.

(continued)

To make the cookie dough: In a medium bowl, sift the flour, baking powder, and salt together. Whisk to combine.

In the bowl of an electric mixer, cream the butter and sugar until thoroughly blended, stopping the mixer once or twice to scrape down the bowl with a rubber spatula. Add the egg and beat until incorporated. Add the vanilla. Scrape the bowl again and mix for a few more seconds. On low speed, add half the dry ingredients. Beat until combined. Add the remaining dry ingredients and beat just until they are completely absorbed into the dough.

Turn the dough out onto a work surface. Gather it together and gently knead into a smooth mass. Flatten it into a disk and cover with plastic wrap. Refrigerate for at least 2 hours or up to 3 days.

Preheat the oven to 350°F. Let the dough sit at room temperature, still covered, for about 20 minutes to soften slightly. On a lightly floured surface, roll the dough to slightly more than $1/8$ inch thick. Using cookie cutters, cut out shapes as close together as possible. Using smaller cutters, cut out a shape from the center of each larger shape. Using a metal spatula or palette knife, transfer the "frames" to ungreased heavy rimless baking sheets, placing them at least $1/2$ inch apart. Place the cut-out centers on the baking sheets as well. (They make charming smaller cookies that look nice on the plate with the stained-glass cookies.)

Gather the dough scraps together; roll and cut the remaining dough. Transfer those shapes to the baking sheets as well. Discard the remaining scraps.

For extra glitter, lightly moisten the surface of the cookies with water using a damp pastry brush. Sprinkle generously with coarse turbinado sugar, if you like.

The dough takes longer to bake than the candy takes to melt in the oven, so bake the cookies first, one sheet at a time, for 15 to 17 minutes, or until the edges begin to turn golden. Remove from the oven, leaving the oven on. To make holes for hanging the cookies, pierce them with the blunt side of a bamboo skewer when they're hot from the oven.

Let the cookies cool for 5 to 10 minutes, then remove them from the baking sheets. Wipe the baking sheets clean and line them with aluminum foil or parchment paper. Reposition the cookies onto the baking sheets (they can be very close together). Mound the open spaces with the pulverized candy, filling them completely. Use the tip of a paring knife to guide the candy pieces. For large open areas, heap the candy so that the "glass" will be sturdy. Place the cookies back in the oven until the candy is liquefied, about 5 minutes. Remove from the oven and let cool completely on the baking sheets. Slide a spatula underneath to release the cookies and store in a cool, dry place.

To do ahead: The wrapped dough may also be frozen for up to 1 month. If the weather is dry, make the Sweet Amber Glass up to 3 days ahead.

palmiers

Caramelized sugar is what gives these light, flaky puff pastry cookies their characteristic crunch and gleaming golden-sugar veneer.

Depending on your imagination, these cookies resemble either unfurled palm leaves or the ears of an elephant. You may have seen them in pastry shops and wondered how they get their shape. The process is easy: Thinly rolled puff pastry dough is folded and layered with lots of sugar. As the cookies bake and spread open, the sugar between the layers of dough caramelizes to a golden crisp. Don't be put off by the quantity of sugar rolled into the dough. It may seem like an inordinate amount, but it's really no more than in any other cookie.

I've made palmiers (pronouned pal-mee-ays) with granulated sugar, confectioners' sugar, brown sugar, and turbinado sugar. They all work well, but I prefer the first two. Confectioners' sugar results in the lightest, airiest version, but you need to add more of it than the other sugars. Granulated sugar makes the cookie a little crunchier.

This recipe calls for store-bought frozen puff pastry. (Feel free to make your own if you're ambitious.) It's generally sold in 17-ounce packages containing 2 sheets of folded dough. One sheet will make 2 dozen cookies.

Makes about twenty-four 2-inch cookies

3/4 cup granulated sugar, or 1 cup confectioners' sugar
1 sheet (8 ounces) frozen puff pastry, thawed

Measure the sugar into a small bowl. Heavily scatter a work surface with some of the sugar. (If using confectioners' sugar, sift rather than sprinkle it over the table and dough.) Unfold the puff pastry and place the rectangle on the sugar. Heavily sprinkle or sift the surface of the dough with more sugar. Using a rolling pin, lightly roll the dough out to a 10-by-15-inch rectangle. Flip the dough once as you roll, adding more sugar as you go. The dough should be about 1/8 inch thick when you finish. Position the dough so that the long ends are at the top and bottom.

Using a pastry brush dipped in water, lightly moisten a 1/2-inch border along the top and bottom edge of the dough. Scatter or sift most of the remaining sugar over the surface of the dough. Fold in the top and bottom edges of the rectangle so they meet in the center. Pat it with your hands to flatten the edges. The rectangle will now be about 5 by 15 inches. Again use the pastry brush to lightly moisten the top and bottom edge of the dough. Sprinkle sugar over the dough and lightly roll across it to press in the sugar. Fold the top half over to meet the bottom edge. You will end up with a long, thick rectangle measuring about 2 1/2 by 15 inches. Using a sharp knife, cut the rectangle in half. Sprinkle any remaining sugar over the surface and gently roll over the top and bottom of each piece, being careful not to deform the shape.

(continued)

palmiers *continued*

Place the 2 pieces of wrapped dough in the freezer
for at least 20 minutes or up to 1 day. Preheat the oven
to 375° F. Line 2 baking sheets with parchment paper or
aluminum foil.

Remove 1 piece of dough from the freezer and, using a
sharp knife, cut it into $1/2$-inch-thick slices. Place
the slices at least 2 inches apart on the prepared baking
sheet so that the cut sides—where the layers are visible—
are facing up. The cookies will fan open.

Bake for about 15 minutes, or until the cookies begin
to turn golden. Remove the baking sheet from the oven
and, using a metal spatula, quickly flip each cookie.
Bake for another 5 minutes, or until golden brown. Let
the cookies cool on the baking sheet for 5 minutes,
then transfer to wire racks to cool completely. Repeat
to bake the remaining cookies. If you're reusing the
same baking sheet, let it cool completely before baking
the next batch.

To do ahead: Freeze the rolled dough for up to 1 day,
wrapped in plastic wrap.

Candy
and confections

As an opulent end to a lavish meal or a heartfelt gift to a friend, homemade candy is a delightful frivolity. Candy making mainly consists of watching a pot boil. The entire process takes place on the stove. Aside from good ingredients, the most important requirements are a heavy saucepan, an accurate thermometer, a wooden spatula, and a watchful eye.

The basis of the confectioner's craft lies in understanding the behavior of sugar when heated. Sugar melts into syrup when combined with a liquid such as water, cream, or melted butter. As it boils, moisture evaporates, leaving a greater concentration of sugar and dairy solids. The less moisture remaining, the higher the thermometer will climb. Cooled to room temperature, the sugar syrup will set up to varying degrees of hardness, depending on how much moisture is left. From a chewy, soft caramel—which cooks to 244°F—to the glasslike shatter of brittle—which cooks to more than 300°F—sugar magically transforms itself.

Tips for Making Candy

• Read "Caution: Hot Caramel," page 19.

• Cook candy in a heavy saucepan. Dairy products such as butter and cream, which are often added to the pan, can easily scorch.

• Use the size of saucepan called for in the recipe. When sugar is boiled with cream or butter, it foams and bubbles, rising quite high in the pan. You need a saucepan deep enough to prevent it from overflowing. (This is also the reason many recipes call for adding the cream in stages: once some of the liquid has boiled off, there is room in the pan for more.) On the other hand, a pan shouldn't be too large. If the level of liquid is too low, the thermometer can't accurately register. To determine the capacity of a saucepan, fill it with a measured amount of water.

• Wash down the sides of the pan with a wet pastry brush to dissolve any clinging sugar crystals, as when cooking any caramel. Don't add any more water than is necessary, however, as excess liquid will prolong the cooking time.

• Candy recipes containing fatty ingredients such as butter and heavy cream often call for warming the sugar solution over low heat before allowing it to boil. Fat tends to prevent sugar from dissolving easily. Warming the mixture first gives the sugar crystals in the high-fat solution extra time to melt.

• Use a slow, steady figure-8 motion to stir the ingredients, scraping along the corners of the pot. A wooden spatula with a flat edge works best. The high heat will melt a rubber spatula; a metal spoon will conduct heat to your hand.

• Some candy, such as brittle and buttercrunch, can be cooked until it reaches the desired shade of amber; let your eyes be your guide. Caramels, on the other hand, must be cooked to the exact temperature called for in a recipe. A few degrees either way can make the difference between a caramel that is too soft or too hard.

• If at all possible, use a digital candy/fat thermometer, available through Williams-Sonoma (800-541-2233). It's more accurate than a mercury thermometer, and easier to read. (To get a true reading with a mercury thermometer, stoop so that your eyes are level with the numbers.) Position the thermometer so that it's slightly raised off the bottom of the pot. To test a thermometer, place it in a pot of boiling water; it should read 212°F.

• When the candy has reached the desired temperature, *immediately remove it from the heat.* The sugar will continue to cook from the residual heat in the pan. Even a turned-off burner adds too much heat.

• Once cooked, pour the molten candy onto a heavy baking sheet or into a heavy pan. (The high heat will buckle thin metal.) For pouring brittle and buttercrunch, read about parchment paper and silicone mats, on page 12. When molding caramels in a pan, it's preferable to use a heavy metal pan with completely square corners, as opposed to a glass dish with rounded corners. You can find them in most fine cookware stores. (They also come in handy for baking brownies and molding marshmallows.)

• To package or present candy, I like to use "natural" waxed paper, which can be found in gourmet food stores, natural foods stores, and even some supermarkets. The pale brown color harmonizes nicely with the golden color of brittle, toffee, and caramels. Tear sheets off the roll to layer the candy in tins, or cut the paper into smaller pieces for wrapping individual candies. Natural-colored waxed paper bags also make terrific packaging for shards of buttercrunch and brittle. Soft individual candies such as turtles and caramel clusters are often placed in glassine candy cups to prevent them from sticking to one another. See page 12 for candy-packaging sources.

• The texture of caramels and toffee improves within a day or so. Although they contain dairy products, there is little chance of these candies spoiling because the ingredients are boiled for so long, at so high a temperature. They may, however, dry out as moisture evaporates (in the case of some caramels) or change in texture as the sugar slowly crystallizes over time (as with toffee and buttercrunch). Brittle absorbs moisture from the air and becomes tacky if the atmosphere is damp. The ideal conditions for making and keeping candy are in the cooler, drier months. Happily, that is when we most feel like eating sweets and gifting treats.

Using Chocolate

Chocolate and caramel are uniquely suited to each other. The slightly bitter undertone of dark chocolate is a pleasing contrast to the sweet finish of caramel candies. For those of us who love chocolate as an accent flavor rather than a main ingredient, it's perfect to round out and complete the flavor of confections such as caramels, turtles, nut clusters, and buttercrunch.

Use only the best chocolate for dipping and coating your homemade candy. High-quality chocolate bars—scored for easy measuring—are readily available. Supermarkets carry 4-ounce bars of bittersweet and semisweet Ghirardelli chocolate. Slim bars of Lindt and Valrhona chocolate, along with large bars of Callebaut, are sold in gourmet grocery stores.

The terms *bittersweet* and *semisweet* are relative; there are no official standards. What one company labels as bittersweet could contain more sugar than another brand's semisweet. Let your taste buds be your guide. If milk chocolate is your choice, by all means substitute it in any candy recipe here calling for semisweet or bittersweet chocolate. Milk chocolate, however, contains more sugar than dark chocolate. Keep in mind that the chocolate used for dipping and coating will be combined with candy that is already quite sweet.

Melting Chocolate

Melting chocolate is not difficult, but there are two important rules: First, the chocolate cannot come in contact with any droplets of water, or it will thicken and seize. The container you melt it in and the tool you stir it with must be thoroughly dry. Second, chocolate should be melted slowly, using low heat. Be vigilant. Chocolate burns easily. Scorched chocolate is gritty and smells burnt. It can't be salvaged; throw it out and start over.

Microwave method: Melting chocolate in a microwave is quicker and cleaner than using a double boiler, and it eliminates the possibility of contact with water. When you set the timer, err on the side of caution to prevent burning the chocolate. It's not necessary to finely chop the chocolate—just break it into large pieces. Put the pieces in a dry plastic container or glass bowl. A 1- or 2-cup container is sufficient for melting 4 to 8 ounces of chocolate. Nuke on medium power for about 1 minute. Check the chocolate to see how much is melted by stirring with a rubber spatula—chocolate can fool the eye by retaining its shape even when it is fully melted. Once stirred, microwave again for about 45 seconds until only a few lumps remain. Remove and stir occasionally until the chocolate is smooth and completely melted. You may need to adjust the timing according to your microwave.

Double-boiler method: Place a small stainless-steel bowl over a small saucepan containing an inch of *barely simmering water*. Be sure the bowl doesn't touch the water. Chop the chocolate into small, even pieces. Put it in the bowl and stir occasionally with a rubber spatula until three-quarters of the chocolate is melted. Remove the bowl from the pan and wipe the bottom dry. Stir occasionally with the rubber spatula until completely melted.

Tempering Chocolate

Bars of chocolate used for baking or eating out of hand come from the factory already tempered. Tempering is a process of gently agitating and cooling melted chocolate to a temperature at which the crystals of cocoa butter are stabilized so that they don't separate and float to the surface. When tempered chocolate sets, it has a gleaming, shiny appearance; it stays firm at warm room temperature; and it breaks with a crisp, hard snap.

In order to work with chocolate, it must be melted so that it is liquid. Melting chocolate "knocks it out of temper." It must be retempered before candy is dipped or coated. If not, the chocolate will harden on the candy with a dull finish streaked with gray lines of cocoa butter. The chocolate will melt in your hand, not in your mouth. Don't be intimidated by tempering. It's a simple method of melting, cooling, and gently stirring the chocolate.

There are a number of ways to temper chocolate. Probably the easiest for home use is to reserve about one-third of the chocolate and melt the remainder in either a microwave or double boiler until completely smooth. Finely chop the portion you set aside. Stir the finely chopped chocolate into the melted chocolate. Continue to stir occasionally (and gently) until all the lumps are melted and the chocolate feels cool to the touch when dabbed on the skin just below your lower lip. (The skin below your lip is particularly sensitive to temperature.) For the small amounts of chocolate used in these recipes, this method of testing temperature works well. If you plan to temper a lot of chocolate, you might want to invest in a chocolate thermometer. Purchase it at a cake decorating or cookware store, or through N.Y. Cake & Baking Distributors. (800-942-2539). The temperature of tempered chocolate is about 90°F for dark chocolate and about 88°F for milk chocolate.

Work quickly once the chocolate is tempered—there is a small window of opportunity here. If the chocolate becomes too cool, it will thicken and be difficult to work with.

any nut brittle

Peanut brittle is a classic American confection. To make it, sugar is cooked to the hard-crack stage—a beautiful amber color—and nuts are added. While still warm, the candy is stretched and pulled slightly to make it thin enough to see through in places. The name says it all: When the sugar cools, it's as brittle as thin ice. A small amount of baking soda lends the candy its distinctive porous texture.

While peanuts are traditional, any nut can be encased in brittle. My favorite is pine nuts. Natural foods stores are a good place to buy nuts in bulk. I prefer to use toasted nuts, which are added at the end when the sugar is caramelized. To make brittle with raw nuts, they must cook in the sugar syrup. Add them once the sugar comes to a boil and stir frequently to prevent the nuts from scorching on the bottom of the pot.

To ensure a light-textured brittle, the baking soda must be fresh. An open box that's been sitting on the shelf for some time may still be active, but won't have full potency. If you can't remember when you bought it, invest in a new box.

For holidays or gift giving, make a few batches of brittle in a row, each featuring a different nut. Served together, the varying tastes, textures, and subtle color differences are quite pleasing. A terrific way to present them is in a long, narrow bread basket lined with unbleached (tan-colored) parchment paper. Stand large shards of brittle upright in the basket.

To make a smaller batch, halve the recipe and cook it in a smaller saucepan. Brittle keeps for weeks in a tightly covered, dry tin, although you'll rarely have the chance to test that fact. Don't make brittle in humid weather; it will turn tacky.

Makes 1½ pounds

2 cups sugar
½ cup water
¼ cup light corn syrup
½ teaspoon salt
2 cups (about 7 ounces) toasted nuts;
   see page 23
1 tablespoon unsalted butter
½ teaspoon baking soda

Lightly butter a heavy baking sheet or line it with a silicone mat or parchment paper.

In a heavy 2- to 3-quart saucepan, gently stir the sugar, water, and corn syrup together. Using a wet pastry brush, wash down the sides of the pan. Add the salt. Bring to a boil over medium-high heat and cook, undisturbed, occasionally washing down the sides of the pan, until the sugar starts to color around the edges. Gently swirl the pan to even out the color and continue to cook until the mixture is medium amber. Immediately remove the pan from the heat.

Stir in the nuts and butter. Wait a few seconds for most of the butter to melt, then stir in the baking soda; it will foam up. Stir again and quickly pour the mixture onto the prepared baking sheet. Using a wooden spatula, spread and flatten the mixture as much as possible.

Let cool until the edges can be handled but the mixture is still warm enough to be pliable. Stretch or pull it out so that the nuts are no more than 1 layer deep and you can see through the candy in spots. Let cool completely, then break into large shards.

(continued)

To do ahead: Store in an airtight container, layered with waxed paper, for up to 2 weeks.

almond brittle: Use toasted whole almonds, either blanched or unblanched. You can also use toasted slivered, sliced, or coarsely chopped almonds, if you prefer.

cashew brittle: Use unsalted roasted cashews. They can often be found in natural foods stores.

harvest brittle: This is a stunning seasonal treat for Halloween or a Thanksgiving dessert spread. Mix 1 cup raw pumpkin seeds, 3/4 cup raw sunflower seeds, and 2 tablespoons raw sesame seeds. Add them to the sugar at the first hint of amber color. Stir frequently to prevent scorching.

hazelnut brittle: Use toasted and skinned hazelnuts (see page 23).

peanut brittle: Use unsalted dry-roasted peanuts.

pecan brittle: Like walnuts, these nuts don't have to be toasted, as long as they're fresh and tasty, but they can be. Use large pieces or halves. Add them at the end of boiling when the sugar is a medium amber.

pine nut brittle: Use untoasted nuts. Add them towards the end of boiling when the sugar is partially colored. Stir constantly to prevent the nuts from scorching on the bottom of the pot. To use toasted pine nuts, add them at the end when the sugar is medium amber in color.

walnut brittle: Walnuts have more flavor when lightly toasted, but it's not necessary. Just be sure they're fresh and tasty. Add them at the end of cooking when the sugar is a medium amber.

◌◌

notes: When raw nuts or seeds are added, it's difficult to judge the color of the sugar because the mixture becomes foamy. To accurately assess the color, drop a small amount of the cooked mixture onto a white plate.

◌◌

To quickly butter a baking sheet, rub it with a stick of cold butter.

◌◌

buttercrunch toffee

If you grew up on the Atlantic coast, chances are there was a boardwalk nearby—and a candy kitchen every few blocks. In those fluorescent-lit shops, a woman with her hair pressed into a net would fill a small box with an assortment of chocolates to eat while "strolling the boards." Buttercrunch is the sweet I most associate with those breezy summer nights.

As in brittle, the sugar here is cooked to a temperature high enough to ensure a crunchy texture. But a significant amount of butter is added to the pan, which softens buttercrunch to a fine-grained candy with a gentle bite. Like brittle, the name buttercrunch *says it all.*

The terms buttercrunch *and* toffee *are often interchangeable. This candy is sold in any number of forms: cut into neat rectangles or squares, or broken into irregular pieces, as it is here. There may be nuts in the toffee, or only on the outside. Chocolate, or not. Here, the toffee slab is coated on one side with dark chocolate and finely chopped nuts.*

Makes about 2 pounds

2 1/4 cups almonds, pecans, or other nuts, finely chopped
1 cup (2 sticks) unsalted butter
2 tablespoons water
2 tablespoons light corn syrup
1 1/2 cups sugar
4 ounces bittersweet or semisweet chocolate, finely chopped

Butter a 9-by-13-inch baking sheet or jelly-roll pan. Line it with aluminum foil so that it extends up the sides, pressing the foil securely into the corners. Lightly butter the foil. Place an unbreakable glass of water next to the stove for storing the pastry brush and wooden spatula or spoon when not in use.

Sprinkle the prepared pan with a layer of nuts, about 1 1/4 cups. In a 2- or 3-quart saucepan, melt the butter over low heat. Add the water and corn syrup and bring it just to a boil. Remove from the heat and stir in the sugar. Using a wet pastry brush, wash down the sides of the pan. Bring it to a boil over medium-high heat. Insert a candy thermometer and, stirring frequently with a figure-8 motion, boil until the temperature reaches 300° F, about 7 minutes. The mixture will appear thick and fluffy and will be pale tan in color.

Pour the toffee into the prepared pan and use the wooden spatula to evenly spread it to the edges. Let cool for 3 minutes, then sprinkle the finely chopped chocolate over the surface of the toffee. When it melts (the chocolate will maintain its form even when melted; poke a "chunk" with your finger to test), use an offset metal spatula to evenly spread the chocolate to the edges. Sprinkle with the remaining nuts. Refrigerate the buttercrunch for about 20 minutes, then let sit at room temperature until the chocolate is completely firm.

Ideally, buttercrunch should mellow at room temperature for at least 12 hours before serving, to develop a fine-grained texture. Break it into irregular pieces.

To do ahead: Store in an airtight container, layered with waxed paper, for up to 2 weeks.

classic cream caramels

It's amazing to me that a pan of sugar, cream, and butter can transform itself into golden, chewy caramel candies simply by boiling away on the stove. The true flavor of caramel candies comes not only from caramelized sugar, but from a reaction that takes place between the dairy protein and the reducing sugars (corn syrup or honey), known as the Maillard reaction.

Because milk has a higher protein content than cream, it produces a tastier caramel. But milk is 88 percent water: It takes a lot of cooking to evaporate all that moisture. Sweetened condensed milk contains all the protein, but only 28 percent water. The caveat is that it burns easily. Here, I've developed a rich, flavorful caramel that contains both heavy cream and condensed milk. The latter is added toward the end so there is less chance of scorching. Nonetheless, once it's added, stir constantly in a figure-8 motion using a wooden spatula. Maurice Jeffery, teacher and consultant to the confectionery industry, grades his students on how few brown specks there are in a batch.

Fine cookware stores often carry a 9-inch square pan, 2 inches high, which has squared-off corners (as opposed to glass dishes, which have rounded corners). This type of pan is especially good for molding caramels.

Makes 2 3/4 pounds

2 cups sugar
1/2 cup water
1 1/2 cups light corn syrup
1/2 teaspoon salt
1/2 cup (1 stick) unsalted butter, cut into pieces
2 cups heavy cream
1 cup sweetened condensed whole milk (see notes)
1 tablespoon pure vanilla extract

Line a 9-inch square pan with aluminum foil so that the edges of the foil are overhanging; press the foil snugly into the corners of the pan. Lightly butter the foil. Set the prepared pan on a cooling rack. Place a nonbreakable glass of water next to the stove for storing the pastry brush and wooden spatula when not in use.

In a 3 1/2- or 4-quart saucepan, gently stir the sugar, water, corn syrup, and salt together. Wash down the sides of the pan with a wet pastry brush. Over medium-high heat, bring the syrup to a boil. Insert a candy thermometer and boil, undisturbed, until the temperature reaches 250°F, about 7 minutes. Wash down the sides of the pan and add the butter. Once it melts, gradually stir in 1 cup of the heavy cream; bring to a boil (see notes). In about 5 minutes, when the level of liquid reduces somewhat, gradually stir in the remaining 1 cup cream. Continue to boil, stirring occasionally with a figure-8 motion, until the temperature reaches 250°F, about 7 minutes.

(continued)

Remove the pan from the heat and stir in the condensed milk. Return the pan to the heat. Stirring *constantly* with a figure-8 motion, boil until the temperature reaches 244° F, about 4 minutes. Immediately remove from the heat and continue to stir for 1 minute. Stir in the vanilla. Pour the caramel into the prepared pan without scraping the saucepan.

Let the caramel cool and sit, undisturbed, for at least 8 hours or as long as overnight; do not cover. Turn the caramel out onto a piece of waxed or parchment paper and peel off the foil. Using a large sharp knife, cut the slab into quarters. Cut each quarter into four 1-by-4-inch bars or into sixteen 1-inch squares or 1/2-by-2-inch rectangles.

To do ahead: Store the caramels, wrapped, at room temperature, for up to 3 weeks.

honey vanilla walnut caramels: With undercurrents of aromatic honey, vanilla bean, and large walnut pieces, these soft, smooth caramels are superb. In fact, they're my favorites.

Follow the recipe for Classic Cream Caramels, substituting 1/2 cup honey for 1/2 cup of the corn syrup. Add the honey along with the remaining cup of corn syrup. Cook to 245° F (1° higher than Classic Cream Caramels). Remove from the heat and stir in 2 cups lightly toasted walnuts along with 1 tablespoon vanilla extract and the seeds scraped from a vanilla bean. Pour into the prepared pan and let cool for at least 8 hours. Cut the slab into quarters and each quarter into squares or bars.

chocolate-dipped caramels: It may be gilding the lily, but a dip of dark chocolate on the tip of a chewy golden caramel is the ultimate treat. Cut the caramels into squares or rectangles. Or, use a small cookie cutter to cut out caramel hearts. (For minimal waste, cut the shapes as close together as possible, reversing the direction of the heart cutter each time.)

Using a sharp knife, cut the Classic Cream Caramels into desired shapes. Line a baking sheet with parchment paper or a silicone mat. Grasping a caramel by the top edges, dip the bottom in 8 ounces tempered semisweet or bittersweet chocolate (see page 118), allowing the chocolate to come halfway up the sides of the candy. (It's easier to dip rectangles if the chocolate is placed in a small flat-bottomed container.) Slide the bottom of the dipped caramel along the edge of the chocolate bowl to lightly scrape off any excess. Caramel squares can also be dipped diagonally, from corner to corner.

Place the dipped caramel on the prepared baking sheet. If properly tempered, the chocolate should set within 5 minutes at room temperature. Place the baking sheet in the refrigerator for 5 to 15 minutes. Slide a small palette knife under each candy to release it and avoid getting fingerprints on the chocolate.

notes: Be sure to use *sweetened condensed whole milk* when making caramels. It is lower in sugar than sweetened condensed *skim* milk and much lower in water content than evaporated milk. A 14-ounce can of sweetened condensed milk contains about $1^1/_3$ cups.

To prevent the pot from boiling over when making caramels, the cream is added in stages. Cream rises in a bubbly froth as it boils—it would require a very large pot to cook a relatively small amount of candy. By adding it gradually, the liquid has time to evaporate and reduce, concentrating and caramelizing the solids, making room for the next cup of cream.

Unless you have someone helping you dip, you may want to temper only 4 ounces of chocolate at a time. Otherwise, the chocolate may cool and thicken before you finish dipping all the pieces.

wrapping caramels

There is no sweeter gift to give than a box of homemade caramels. Making them is simple. Wrapping them, however, is a labor of love. Use "natural" waxed paper (which is a pretty pale brown color and can be found in gourmet or natural foods stores) or cellophane to prevent the pieces from sticking together. The easiest way to individually wrap caramels is to twist the ends of the wrapper like salt-water taffy. Rectangular caramels are easier to wrap than squares. Once twisted, trim the ends with scissors to even.

A good shortcut is to cut the slab of caramel into 1-by-4-inch bars rather than individual pieces. Wrap each bar in waxed paper or cellophane and twist the ends, You can even secure the twisted ends with thin ribbon or thread. To create a decorative edge on the twisted ends, use pinking shears to cut the waxed paper before wrapping the candy. A charming way to serve a log of caramel is to place it on a wooden cutting board along with a small knife and pass it around the table.

turtles

They're so easy to make, it's surprising these sweet little critters are rarely made at home. Taking their name from their shape, turtles are formed by dropping dollops of soft, chewy caramel onto a bed of pecans. Each caramel is then topped with a round of chocolate, either milk or dark—as you like.

Turtles make a terrific gift. For my wedding, I piped chocolate hearts onto the caramel and stacked two "Turtle Hearts" in a little box as a favor for each guest. To package, place the turtles in glassine candy cups to prevent them from sticking to each other.

This recipe calls for a large quantity of nuts to be spread thickly in a jelly-roll pan. In the end, you'll use only about half of the nuts, but it's easier to drop the caramel onto a solid blanket of nuts, rather than onto separate clusters. You will have twice as much Creamy Caramel Coating as you need. To double the amount of turtles, fill 2 jelly-roll pans with nuts and use all of the caramel.

Makes 26 to 28 turtles

6 cups (1¹/₃ pounds) pecan halves
Creamy Caramel Coating (page 26),
  cooked to 238°F
4 ounces good-quality semisweet or
  milk chocolate, tempered (see page 118)

Line a 10-by-15-inch jelly-roll pan with aluminum foil; lightly butter the foil. Evenly spread the pecans in the bottom of the prepared pan and pat them with the palm of your hand to level them as much as possible. Butter the front and back of 2 teaspoons. Make the caramel.

Set the hot caramel aside to cool until thick but still fluid, about 5 minutes. Using one of the buttered spoons, scoop about ¹/₂ spoonful of caramel and use the other buttered spoon to slide it onto the pecans. It should spread to about the size of a quarter. (If too runny, let the caramel cool a little longer.) Repeat with the remaining caramel, spacing the drops so that they don't touch. If the caramel becomes too stiff, warm it over low heat, gently stirring. Set the pan aside for the caramel to cool completely.

Using another teaspoon, drop about ¹/₂ spoonful of tempered chocolate onto the caramel. Spread it a little with the back of the spoon if it mounds, but let the caramel show all around the edges of the chocolate. (Leftover chocolate can be reused at another time.) Refrigerate until the chocolate is set, about 15 minutes.

Lift each turtle and pull out any pecans that are barely attached. The pecans remaining in the tray can be reused: There will be about 3 cups left over. Let the turtles come to room temperature before serving.

To do ahead: Make the caramel up to 1 week ahead. Reheat until warm and fluid, but not too thin and runny. Turtles will keep for weeks, but are best eaten within a day or so of making them. Store in an airtight container, layered with aluminum foil or parchment paper or place each in a glassine candy cup. If they stick together, cut apart using lightly buttered scissors.

roadkill turtles (caramel nut clusters):

Small patties of gooey caramel, crunchy nuts, and dark chocolate are essentially turtles without the shape. They're quicker to make, don't require as many nuts, and you can use whatever nut you like.

Line a large baking sheet with parchment paper or a silicone mat. Lightly butter a small bowl and the front and back of 2 teaspoons. Place 1 cup plus 2 table-spoons toasted hazelnuts, almonds, walnuts, or pecans in the buttered bowl. Make Creamy Caramel Coating, bringing the final boil to exactly 238°F. Using a rubber spatula, gently stir half (1 cup) of the hot caramel into the nuts. Using 1 buttered teaspoon, scoop a bite-sized dollop of the caramel-nut mixture and use the other buttered spoon to slide it onto the prepared baking sheet. Repeat with the remaining mixture, dropping the clusters about 1 inch apart. There will be about 26 clusters. Set aside for the caramel to cool completely.

Lift a caramel nut cluster by a protruding nut on top and dip the bottom into the tempered chocolate. Slide the bottom of the dipped cluster along the edge of the chocolate bowl to lightly scrape off any excess. (The leftover chocolate can be reused at another time.) Return to the baking sheet and repeat with the remaining clusters. Refrigerate until the chocolate is set, about 15 minutes. Slide a small palette knife under each candy to release it and to avoid getting fingerprints on the chocolate. Let the caramel clusters come to room temperature before serving. Place each in a glassine candy cup, if you like.

Professional candy makers deposit dollops of warm caramel using a metal funnel plugged with a wooden stick. The stick is raised and lowered to release the desired amount. It's quicker and cleaner than spooning the caramel. Funnels can be purchased in most cookware stores. Lightly oil the inside of the funnel and the wooden stick to prevent the caramel from sticking. Also, the tempered chocolate can be piped onto the caramel using a pastry bag. Between turtles, plug the tip of the bag with your finger to stop the flow of chocolate.

golden ladies

This is a grown-up version of a kiddie classic: caramel apples on a stick. These diminutive treats are easy to get your mouth around. Little red Lady apples, sweet Seckel pears, or miniature green Forelle pears are dipped by their stems into thick golden caramel, then coated with a band of bittersweet chocolate.

Golden Ladies are a perfect end to an autumn dinner party. They're also terrific on a Halloween buffet or at the Thanksgiving table, presented on a pedestal cake stand.

Choose fruit with stems long enough to grasp; a clinging leaf adds charm. For a more rustic look, skewer the stem ends with twigs you collect in the woods.

Makes 16 to 18

16 to 18 Lady apples, Seckel pears,
    and/or Forelle pears (about 3 pounds) with
    sturdy stems
Double recipe Creamy Caramel Coating (page 26)
    cooked to 240°F
6 to 8 ounces semisweet or bittersweet chocolate,
    tempered (see page 118)

If you wash the fruit, be sure it is dry. Lightly butter a heavy baking sheet or line it with a silicone mat or parchment paper. Make the caramel.

To dip the fruit: Tilt the pot of caramel and, grasping a fruit by the stem, submerge it in the hot caramel, leaving a border around the stem uncovered to reveal the natural colors of the fruit. Let the caramel drip back into the pot for a few seconds, then gently scrape the bottom of the fruit along the edge of the pot to remove any excess. Hold the fruit upside down for a few seconds to set the caramel. (The idea is to cool it just long enough to prevent a "foot" from forming around the bottom.) Stand the fruit up on the prepared baking sheet and repeat with the remaining pieces. As the level of caramel lowers, tilt the pot at a greater angle and rotate the fruit to cover. When the caramel becomes too stiff, stir it gently over low heat to rewarm; do not let it boil. Let the coated fruit cool completely.

Pour the tempered chocolate into a small bowl or cup. (The smaller and deeper the container, the easier it is to dip the fruit.) Grasping the fruit by the stem, dip it into the chocolate so that it comes about halfway up the caramel. Scrape the bottom of the fruit along the edge of the container to remove any excess chocolate. Place the fruit back on the prepared baking sheet. Repeat with the remaining fruit. Refrigerate the fruit for about 10 minutes to set the chocolate. Be careful not to jostle the pan or the chocolate bottoms will smear. When the chocolate is set, the fruit will lift easily off the baking sheet. Serve at room temperature within 6 hours.

To do ahead: Make the Creamy Caramel Coating up to 1 week ahead and refrigerate. When ready to dip the fruit, warm the caramel over low heat, stirring, or in the microwave for less than 1 minute.

caramel-coated sliced and whole apples: For an easy-to-eat party alternative, slice medium apples and dip each piece more than halfway into Creamy Caramel Coating; roll the ends in chopped pecans or walnuts. To dip apples, skewer them first with wooden sticks; let the coated apples set, upside-down, on a baking sheet lined with parchment paper. This recipe will cover 6 to 8 medium apples.

caramel popcorn

The last time I ate caramel popcorn from a box, I was more intent on digging for the prize than I was on eating the contents.

This caramel popcorn tastes better than any I remember. Buttery brown sugar caramel lightly coats every nook and cranny of each crunchy kernel. The only problem is, it's impossible to stop eating. Extremely simple to make, this is terrific party food.

I'm a purist: I prefer this made with popcorn only. But to add nuts, substitute 2 cups of unsalted roasted peanuts or toasted pecans or almonds for an equal measure of popcorn. To form popcorn balls, gently press them into shape while still warm from the oven.

Makes about 12 cups

12 cups popped popcorn
1 cup packed light brown sugar
1/4 cup light corn syrup
1/2 teaspoon salt
1/2 cup (1 stick) unsalted butter
1/2 teaspoon baking soda

Place an unbreakable glass of water next to the stove for storing the pastry brush and wooden spatula when not in use. Lightly butter a large roasting pan and wooden spatula. Preheat the oven to 200°F. Place the popcorn in the prepared pan. (If adding nuts, toss them in.)

In a 6-cup saucepan, stir the brown sugar, corn syrup, and salt together. Wash down the sides of the pot with a wet pastry brush. Add the butter and cook over low heat until the butter melts. Do not let it boil until the butter is melted.

On medium-high heat, bring the mixture to a boil. Stir it, wash down the sides of the pan with the wet pastry brush, and insert a candy thermometer. Boil until the temperature reaches 250°F, 4 to 5 minutes.

Remove from the heat. Wait about 20 seconds and stir in the baking soda; it will foam up. Quickly pour the caramel over the popcorn and, using the buttered spatula, stir gently until all the kernels are coated.

Bake for 1 hour, turning the mixture twice during that time. Be sure to scrape along the bottom of the pan with the spatula to bring up all the caramel. Turn out into a large bowl. To prevent the kernels from sticking together, stir and separate the popcorn a few times as it cools. Serve slightly warm or at room temperature.

To do ahead: Store in a tightly covered tin for up to 2 days.

mad caps

These confections are inspired by a Coney Island candy stand, Philip's, formerly at the end of the subway line in Brooklyn. They made caramel-coated marshmallows on a stick—which is the perfect way to eat them when you're strolling the boardwalk.

Here, marshmallows are double-dipped, one end in chocolate and the other in gooey caramel. These tricolored treats make charming "petits fours" for a party. Whether served on a Halloween buffet or at the end of a Passover seder, even the most sophisticated "foodie" falls for these fun and irresistible caramel treats.

You can also forego the chocolate bottoms. If you do, dip the marshmallows deeper. When they set, place them in gold-foil candy cups or stack 2 or 3 on a bamboo skewer—as they did at Philip's. Be sure to use soft marshmallows from a freshly opened bag.

Makes about 40 marshmallows

6 ounces good-quality bittersweet or semisweet chocolate, tempered (see page 118)
10-ounce bag marshmallows
Creamy Caramel Coating, (page 26) cooked to 235°F

Line 2 baking sheets with parchment paper or silicone mats. Temper the chocolate in a small bowl or microwave container. Holding a marshmallow by one end, dip it into the chocolate, covering the bottom and about $1/4$ inch up the sides. Shake it and scrape any excess chocolate off on the edge of the bowl as you lift it. Place the marshmallow, chocolate-side down, on the prepared baking sheet. Repeat with the remaining marshmallows. Work quickly so that the chocolate doesn't harden before you are done. Refrigerate until the chocolate is set, 5 to 15 minutes. If properly tempered and fully set, they will adhere slightly to the parchment paper, but will lift off cleanly, without leaving a mark. Slide a small palette knife under each marshmallow first to release it. Any leftover chocolate can be reused.

To dip the marshmallow tops in the caramel:
The caramel should be thick and fluid, but not runny. If too cool and stiff, heat it in the microwave or over low heat, stirring occasionally, until barely warm to the touch. Grasping the chocolate end of the marshmallow with your fingers, dip the top half in about $1/2$ inch; shake gently to remove any excess. Set the marshmallow, caramel top up, back on the baking sheet. (If the caramel drips down the sides of the marshmallow, it is too warm.) There should be a stripe of white marshmallow between the chocolate and the caramel. Repeat with the remaining marshmallows. If the caramel becomes too stiff, gently rewarm. Serve the same day. There will be leftover caramel, which can be reused.

To do ahead: Make the Creamy Caramel Coating up to 1 week ahead and refrigerate. When ready to dip the marshmallows, warm the caramel over low heat, stirring, or in the microwave for less than 1 minute.

Ornaments
and accessories

Also see: Fresh Fruit in Amber Candy Coating, page 38

Taking advantage of the fact that molten caramel can be dripped, drizzled, or poured, we can make all sorts of glitzy, golden ornaments and accessories that add glamour to any dessert.

Except for decorations that are poured, such as Cutouts and Nuggets, the caramel should be slightly cool and thick so that it can be controlled. Plunge the bottom of the hot pan into ice water for a few seconds to stop the cooking. When the caramel becomes too cool to work with, simply reheat it.

Tips for Making Caramel Decorations

· Cook the caramel only until it is light amber in color, as it will darken somewhat when it's reheated.

· Plunge the bottom of the pan into ice water for a few seconds as soon as the caramel reaches the desired color. This arrests the cooking process so that the caramel does not continue to darken.

· Water dissolves caramel, so be sure the work area is dry. Once the cooking pan is removed from the ice water, wipe the bottom dry to ensure that no water accidentally drips onto the work surface.

· Caramel stiffens as it cools, making it difficult to work with. To maintain a molten consistency while you're making decorations, rewarm it over the lowest possible heat. If the caramel starts to boil, it's too hot; remove the pan from the burner for a few minutes, then replace it when the caramel becomes too thick and cool.

· Caramel decorations will keep their shape for days—even weeks—in a cool, dry environment, but will wilt, sag, or melt within hours in hot, humid weather. In dry weather, store them on layers of parchment or waxed paper until ready to use. They are good for as long as they hold their shape.

· To have caramel for decorations on hand at all times, make it ahead and melt it as you need it: Pour the hot caramel in a puddle onto a baking sheet lined with parchment paper or a silicone mat. When it cools, break it into pieces and place in an airtight container. It will keep for days, weeks, or months, depending on the weather. To reuse, simply place pieces of caramel in a saucepan and reheat over low heat, stirring occasionally, until fluid. You can keep adding more caramel to the pan as you need it. Unless it becomes too dark, any leftover caramel can be reused.

basic recipe for caramel decorations

The method for caramelizing sugar is the same for all of the following recipes. Double or triple the recipe if you need extra decorations.

Makes 1 cup

1 cup sugar
¼ cup water
½ teaspoon fresh lemon juice

Prepare the baking sheet or utensils according to directions in each recipe. Fill a bowl large enough to accommodate the bottom of the pan halfway with ice water.

To make the caramel: In a small saucepan, gently stir the sugar, water, and lemon juice together. Using a wet pastry brush, wash down the sides of the pan. Bring to a boil over medium-high heat until the sugar starts to color around the edges. Gently swirl the pan to even out the color and continue to cook the mixture until it turns a light amber. Immediately remove the pan from the heat.

Plunge the bottom into the bowl of ice water for about 8 seconds to stop the cooking. Remove the pan from the water and wipe the bottom dry. Discard the ice water.

To do ahead: If the weather is dry, store the decorations, uncovered, at room temperature for an indefinite length of time on a baking sheet lined with parchment paper or aluminum foil. They will sag and melt within hours if it is wet or humid.

coils, curls, and corkscrews

These curlicues add a note of whimsy to a plated dessert. They're fun to make; no two turn out alike. Warm, pliable caramel is pulled into thin strands and coiled around a dowel or the handle of a wooden spoon. It quickly hardens into delicate curled springs of amber candy. Stick them in ice cream sundaes or use them to garnish a plate of caramel-roasted fruit.

Makes about 18 curls

Basic Recipe for Caramel Decorations, at left

Lightly oil a baking sheet or line it with a silicone mat or parchment paper. Lightly oil or butter 2 or 3 dowels of assorted diameters around which you can curl strands of caramel. (I use the handle of a wooden spoon, a child's rolling pin, and a wooden dowel from the hardware store.)

Pour a few dollops of the caramel, each about 1 inch in diameter, onto the prepared baking sheet. Let cool just enough to handle, then form it into a ball and begin to stretch it into a strand. Curl the end around the dowel and slowly pull it into the strand, wrapping it around the stick as you pull it longer. (If you've ever spun wool, it's a similar action.) Don't coil it too tightly against the stick or it will be difficult to slip off once it cools. Make the coil as long as you can; it usually breaks off at 2 to 6 inches. Some coils will be thick, and some will be thin. When cool, in about 1 minute, slip the coil off the dowel. Meanwhile, repeat with another dollop. Continue to pour and pull dollops of caramel. When the caramel in the pan becomes too cool and thick, rewarm it over low heat, stirring occasionally. Return any broken pieces to the pan to remelt and reuse. Stick a few curlicues on top of a dessert.

golden spun sugar

Spun sugar is caramel's magic trick. As improbable as the fairy tale where straw is spun into gold, molten sugar is flung through the air to create shimmering golden threads.

Form the delicate strands into charming nests to hold berries and cream—a terrific Easter dessert—or drape them around a platter of Meringue Snowballs in Caramel Créme Anglaise (page 98). I've shrouded everything from a five-tier wedding cake to a mountain of profiteroles in a translucent netting of caramel.

It's not difficult to spin sugar, but it is a bit of a production. Hot caramel is swung off the end of a pronged tool (improvise by cutting the looped ends off a whisk). The swinging and flinging can be messy, so cover the floor and counter fronts with newspaper. Make sure the work area is completely dry, as water will melt spun sugar. And don't attempt this in humid weather—the fine threads will mat and droop.

Makes enough to cover 1 large cake or dessert or to create 6 individual nests

Basic Recipe for Caramel Decorations (page 134)

Using wire clippers, cut the curved ends off a metal whisk. Lightly oil 2 wooden dowels. Anchor them to the countertop with packing tape, about 2 feet apart, so that they extend out from the counter about 12 inches.

Let the caramel cool and thicken until it drips off the ends of the whisk in steady threads, rather than small droplets. Dip the whisk into the caramel and wave it across, around, and under the sticks, like skeining yarn. The sugar will spin out in very fine threads. Continue to dip the whisk and spin the caramel until it becomes too cool and thick to work with. Rewarm the caramel over low heat, stirring occasionally.

Every so often, loosely gather the golden threads and gently drape them over or around a centerpiece dessert or cake. Continue dipping, swinging, and reheating the caramel until you have enough spun sugar.

To shape nests: Without compressing the strands any more than necessary, gently curve a mass of the spun sugar into a circle and place it in a custard cup or small bowl to form an individual nest. Leave the spun sugar in the cup until you have enough to make another nest. Once the spun sugar is removed from the cup, it will hold the shape.

To do ahead: In dry weather, spun sugar will last a few days, but it never looks quite as pretty as when just made.

gold dust and nuggets

A sprinkling of these glasslike chunks makes a glittering, glitzy garnish on almost any dessert. They couldn't be simpler to make: Cook the caramel, let it cool, chop it up.

Makes 1 cup

Basic Recipe for Caramel Decorations (page 134)

Lightly oil a baking sheet or line it with a silicone mat or parchment paper. Pour the molten caramel onto the prepared baking sheet. Let cool completely.

Place a large piece of waxed paper on a cutting board. Using a large sharp knife, chop the caramel into pieces the size of peas. This will generate smaller pieces and fine golden powder as well. (Don't take shortcuts like grinding it in a food processor or crushing it with a rolling pin; it will lose its sparkle and luster.)

Sprinkle over a dessert for garnish, being sure to include the dust as well as the larger chunks.

To do ahead: If the nuggets become tacky, remelt the chunks of caramel in a small saucepan over low heat, stirring occasionally. When the caramel liquefies, pour it onto the prepared baking sheet; cool and cut.

note: Nut Praline, coarsely chopped, is essentially Gold Nuggets with nuts. If you want a garnish that is nutty as well as glitzy, use that recipe (page 22).

caramel cutouts

Cookie cutters serve as molds for amber-colored candy decorations. Simply pour a little molten caramel into each, let it cool, then press it out. Hearts of varying sizes are an especially sweet garnish for a Valentine's Day dessert or an anniversary cake. Use cookie cutters that are open on the top and bottom, rather than those that have a solid top.

Makes about 12 shapes

Basic Recipe for Caramel Decorations (page 134)

Spray or brush with oil the insides of about 6 cookie cutters. Lightly oil a baking sheet or line it with a silicone mat or parchment paper. Place the prepared cookie cutters on the baking sheet.

Carefully spoon some molten caramel into each cookie cutter so that it is about ⅛ inch deep. Let cool completely until the caramel is hard. Gently release each from the cutter by spreading the metal slightly or pushing gently on the candy with your fingers. If a caramel shape breaks, hold a broken edge close to a flame for 1 second to melt slightly. Adhere it to the piece from which it broke and hold it in place for a few seconds until it cools and sets. Place the cutouts on and around a cake, custard, or ice cream sundae.

drips, drizzles, and puddles

You can pour, drizzle, or drip molten caramel to make zigzags, spirals, initials, musical notes, or small hearts. Once they harden, use them to decorate cakes, puddings, or ice cream sundaes. Edible caramel swizzle sticks look snazzy in cocktails and kiddie drinks.

Makes about 16 decorations

Basic Recipe for Caramel Decorations (page 134)

Lightly oil a baking sheet or line it with a silicone mat or parchment paper. Use a teaspoon or fork to drip the caramel. Experiment with different shapes. When the caramel in the pan becomes too cool and thick, rewarm it over low heat, stirring occasionally. Return any unsuccessful attempts or broken pieces to the pan to remelt and reuse.

lacy caramel bowls and cages

These lacy golden bowls are a dramatic way to present a simple dessert of berries and cream or scoops of ice cream with caramel sauce. They can also be inverted to create golden cages over individual desserts, such as baked apples, or make one large cage to cover a special cake or centerpiece dessert. Unlike spun sugar bowls, which are gossamer filaments of sugar, these lacy bowls are hard and brittle, like lollipops.

Normally, these bowls and cages are created by drizzling the caramel over the back of an oiled or foil-covered bowl. I find this method frustrating, as the caramel often shatters when the bowl is removed. Here, I've developed a method that not only avoids that problem but takes the panic out of the process.

The caramel is first drizzled onto parchment paper within a traced circle. It's then warmed a few seconds in the oven until pliable, then it's draped over the back of a small bowl so that it molds into shape. If the weather is dry, you can leave the drizzled circles on the parchment paper overnight, and mold them into bowls the following day.

Makes about nine 4-inch bowls

Basic Recipe for Caramel Decorations (page 134)

Clear all the racks out of the oven and preheat it to 400°F. Line a baking sheet with parchment paper and use the mouth of a 6- or 7-inch bowl to trace 2 or 3 circles on the paper. Using a pastry brush, lightly brush the paper with butter; wipe off any excess. Lightly butter the backs of 2 or 3 small bowls or cups; wipe off any excess. These will be the molds for the caramel bowls.

Let the caramel cool and thicken until it drips off a spoon in a continuous thread. Using a teaspoon, drizzle the caramel over the paper in a Jackson Pollock pattern, staying within the drawn circle. The more you drizzle, the sturdier the bowl. Repeat with a second circle. When the caramel in the pot becomes too cool and thick, rewarm it over low heat, stirring occasionally.

When the first circle is cool and brittle, about 3 minutes, gently peel it off by bending back the paper. Open the oven door. Carefully holding the caramel lace round in your hand in the center of the oven, rotate it until it starts to droop—it will only take seconds. Immediately drape the soft round of caramel over the back of a prepared bowl or cup. Let it cool completely while you repeat with the next round. Carefully lift the brittle caramel off the bowl. Fill with ice cream, sorbet, or berries and cream.

To do ahead: Trace as many circles as you will need on parchment paper. Drizzle the caramel inside the drawn circles until you have as many as you want (and a few extras to account for breakage). Very carefully, layer the parchment papers (if you have more than one piece) on a baking sheet and store out of the way in a cool, dry place for an indefinite length of time. The day you plan to serve them, preheat the oven to 400°F and follow the above instructions for heating and molding the lacy rounds. Don't attempt to make these ahead if the weather is humid.

index

index

index

table of equivalents

The exact equivalents in the following tables have been rounded for convenience.

Liquid/Dry Measures

U.S.	Metric
1/4 teaspoon	1.25 milliliters
1/2 teaspoon	2.5 milliliters
1 teaspoon	5 milliliters
1 tablespoon (3 teaspoons)	15 milliliters
1 fluid ounce (2 tablespoons)	30 milliliters
1/4 cup	60 milliliters
1/3 cup	80 milliliters
1/2 cup	120 milliliters
1 cup	240 milliliters
1 pint (2 cups)	480 milliliters
1 quart (4 cups, 32 ounces)	960 milliliters
1 gallon (4 quarts)	3.84 liters
1 ounce (by weight)	28 grams
1 pound	454 grams
2.2 pounds	1 kilogram

Length

U.S.	Metric
1/8 inch	3 millimeters
1/4 inch	6 millimeters
1/2 inch	12 millimeters
1 inch	2.5 centimeters

Oven Temperature

Fahrenheit	Celsius	Gas
250	120	1/2
275	140	1
300	150	2
325	160	3
350	180	4
375	190	5
400	200	6
425	220	7
450	230	8
475	240	9